"Mary Katherine, you're marvelous."

—Ellen DeGeneres

"MK, thank you for cracking us up."

—*TODAY with Hoda & Jenna*

"An infectious laugh that took the internet by storm."

—CNN

"Mary Katherine brings love, wisdom, compassion, humor, and insight to her writing."

—Love What Matters

"Mary Katherine Backstrom's words are so immediately engaging, so filled with humor, and so seemingly effortless, that their depth and insight sneak up on you."

—John Pavlovitz, author, pastor, and activist

"Mary Katherine's message is as infectious as baby goats jumping on trampolines or pet rescue videos. You just can't help but feel optimistic about the world when she is out spreading joy."

—Meredith Ethington, editor-in-chief, *Filter Free Parents*

"MK out here in these streets trying to give out ALL the joy! *Crazy Joy* is the perfect catalyst to finding your footing again in the midst of these insane times."

—TYLER MERRITT, author of *I Take My Coffee Black*

"Mary Katherine is the bomb. In a world of competition and curated perfection, happiness relies on so much. Joy, on the other hand, requires none of those exhausting variables and is exactly what MK turns upside down in *Crazy Joy*. Through MK's humor and seriousness, *Crazy Joy* will inspire you to give up the happy act."

—NATALIE FRANKE, entrepreneur and
author of *Built to Belong*

"If there was ever a person qualified to talk about joy, it's Mary Katherine Backstrom. Even when life is hard, her ability to laugh and make others laugh is impressive. My life has more joy because she's a part of it."

—APRIL AJOY, *Evangelicalish* podcast

"Mary Katherine is a crazy joy genius."

—MEREDITH MASONY, author of *Ask Me What's for Dinner
One More Time*

"What timely and valuable insight from my friend Mary Katherine Backstrom. In a culture that seems so chaotic and uncertain, finding our joy is imperative to being our best selves. MK not only writes it, but she lives it. You can feel her genuine joy for life and relationships whenever you are around her. It's infectious."

—JEREMY COLEMAN, TikTok's "That Pastor from Oklahoma"

"Mary Katherine's writing gives me permission to laugh and cry but also think deeper about what's happening in the world around me."

—KATE SWENSON, founder of Finding Cooper's Voice
and national bestselling author of *Forever Boy*

CRAZY JOY

CRAZY JOY

FINDING *Wild Happiness*
IN A WORLD THAT'S
UPSIDE DOWN

MARY KATHERINE BACKSTROM

WORTHY
PUBLISHING

New York • Nashville

Worthy
Hachette Book Group
1290 Avenue of the Americas, New York, NY 10104
worthypublishing.com
twitter.com/worthypub

Originally published in hardcover and ebook by Worthy in August 2022.
First trade paperback edition: March 2024

Worthy is a division of Hachette Book Group, Inc. The Worthy name and logo are registered trademarks of Hachette Book Group, Inc.

The publisher is not responsible for websites (or their content) that are not owned by the publisher.

The Hachette Speakers Bureau provides a wide range of authors for speaking events. To find out more, go to hachettespeakersbureau.com or email HachetteSpeakers@hbgusa.com.

Worthy Books may be purchased in bulk for business, educational, or promotional use. For information, please contact your local bookseller or the Hachette Book Group Special Markets Department at special.markets@hbgusa.com.

Scripture quotations marked (NIV) are taken from the Holy Bible, New International Version®. Copyright © 1973, 1978,1984, 2011 by Biblica, Inc.™ Used by permission of Zondervan. All rights reserved worldwide. www.zondervan.com. The "NIV" and "New International Version" are trademarks registered in the United States Patent and Trademark Office by Biblica, Inc.™

Print book interior design by Bart Dawson

Library of Congress Control Number: 2022937056

ISBNs: 978-1-5460-1556-7 (trade paperback), 978-1-5460-1553-6 (ebook)

Printed in the United States of America

CW

10 9 8 7 6 5 4 3 2 1

To my wolfpack, Sara & Mer,
who get me in all sorts of trouble,
and Amy, who tries to keep me out of it.

CONTENTS

CRAZY JOY

INTRODUCTION

JOY IN THE JOURNEY

When you are a Bear of Very Little Brain,
and you Think of Things, you find
sometimes that a Thing which seemed
very Thingish inside you is quite different
when it gets out into the open and has
other people looking at it.

—*The House at Pooh Corner*

As we set off together on this journey to joy, there's something you need to know.

I'm just a little bit...*crazy.*

Which is the not-so-politically-correct way of saying that I suffer from mental illness. I've been going to therapy for roughly two decades, and in that time have collected more diagnoses than my son has Pokémon cards. Not that I'm showing off my collection, but (leans in and whispers): It's *impressive*.

Have you ever bought a package of Pokémon cards? You never know what you're going to get. You grab a little blind bag, open the package, and *congratulations*, friend. You are the proud new owner of ten random monsters. Some are cute and some are scary, some are outright weird. And at the top of each card, there's a number that indicates how much damage the monster can do. Me? I have bipolar 2, OCD, PTSD, and some run-of-the-mill ADHD, too. A solid little stable of personal monsters. Damage potential: *high*.

Some days, I wake up and feel like Eeyore, all mopey and clinically depressed. I feel my friendship is a burden to everyone and I'd rather just stay in my house. Other days I wake up bouncing-off-the-walls manic like Tigger, and there's no telling what I might do. I've applied for a job at Medieval Times and bleached the tips of my hair. I've adopted a wild mustang who was aptly named "Trigger" and tore my rotator cuff trying to wrangle him. Mania is a wild ride, but it's kinda-sorta my favorite. There are two polarizing forces competing for space in my head, and mania sure beats the alternative.

If you have no experience with mental illness, this is probably hard to understand. So let me help you out…Imagine you have no choice but to live your life as a character from *Winnie the Pooh*. After weighing the quirks and struggles of each character, would there honestly be any competition?

Nobody would choose to be Mr. Rabbit. He's a narcissistic old coot. Piglet is a porky little anxious mess who needs some Prozac, stat. Maybe you think you would choose to be Pooh, but trust me: That would be a mistake. That whole OCD counting of honey pots would get exhausting pretty darn quick. I assume you've reached the same conclusion as me—that there's only one choice in this game: the bubbliest ray of sunshine in the Hundred Acre Wood. Bouncy, pouncy Tigger.

Tigger is happy. Tigger has energy. Tigger is *manic as hell.*

It seems all of Christopher Robin's friends are in dire need of a therapist.

But hey, who isn't these days?

· · · · · · ·

It was a typical Tuesday therapy session. Me in a cushy leather chair, Dr. C at his mahogany desk. The previous week, I had forgotten my meds, which was a one-way ticket to Tigger Town. Y'all, when I tell you this episode was bad…it damn near ruined my career.

The whole mess started when I fired off a tweet to a local politician. He professes to be a Christian, which I obviously don't hate. But his actions were completely opposite of the gospel, and that is something I *do* hate. The whole thing just infuriated me, so I reached out and told him so. To my surprise, he responded. And his response straight pissed me off.

I worked all night and through lunch the next day, making plans to end his career. By one o'clock the next afternoon, I'd chosen a campaign manager. By three o'clock I'd launched my website. Momma wasn't playing around. Less than a day after our initial exchange, I returned to my Twitter account.

"Good morning, Mr. Congressman. Enjoy your job while it lasts. Your seat comes up in 18 months and I am running to take it."

Yes! This is a great idea, my mania cheered me on. Mentally, my cup was overflowing with ideas and hope and potential. Physically, I had the energy of a thousand suns. Not a single part of me doubted the absolute brilliance of this plan. I sent that tweet out into the universe, then closed the app on my screen.

The tweet went viral, and perhaps I would have cared… but I was no longer interested in politics. I had a newer, shinier plan: I was gonna start a food truck. One that sold buttermilk biscuits. Only buttermilk biscuits. Biscuit sandwiches, biscuit potpies, biscuit shortcake desserts. I didn't need to run for Congress; this boss babe was gonna make millions.

Dr. C listened to all of this quietly, until my story ran out of steam.

"And how did this all work out for you?" he asked. The question was obviously rhetorical.

"Uh…not so great," I replied, which was a bit of an understatement. That week was one continuous cringe. Just remembering it still gives me heartburn. First, a business colleague called a meeting to discuss some "serious concerns." They had valid questions about the direction of my career. Was I suddenly making a change? Was I becoming a divisive political figure? When I signed a contract with this faith-based publisher, they believed my dream was different. The understanding was that I wanted to share hope and laughter and Jesus—not kick political anthills on the internet.

Then, my husband called from work. I'll leave that conversation off the page. Suffice it to say this: If you decide to run for the United States Congress, you should probably tell your life partner first.

"A lot of people were confused and upset," I continued. "And I was honestly humiliated. I deleted the post and cried in bed. I was depressed the whole next week."

Dr. C nodded quietly. "It sounds like your manic episodes are happening more and more." He was right. Even before I skipped my meds, I'd been manic more and more frequently. "Perhaps it's time to consider a mood stabilizer. It could help you balance things out."

I knew this was a reasonable suggestion, but something inside me balked.

"I dunno," I replied. Dr. C raised an eyebrow. "It's hard to explain," I continued. "I know my mania is destructive, but I like the way it makes me feel. I don't want it to go away. It's almost like a drug. For a few days, I believe that everything's possible. I have all the energy in the world. Nobody and nothing can steal my sunshine. It's like I'm high on happiness."

"I understand you want to feel happy," said Dr. C. "But at what cost?"

• • • • • • •

The other day I was digging through an heirloom chest that contained all sorts of memories. Shuffling through yellowed photographs and beat-up Broadway *Playbills*, I discovered a folded-up note. Turning it over in my hands, I felt a pang of nostalgia. Kids nowadays send text messages, DMs, or snaps that disappear after opening. The art of the paper "pull here" tab will die with my generation. It's a shame, too, because there's nothing as hilarious as a love letter written in middle school. But this wasn't a ballad from my childhood sweetheart. And it didn't seem to be from a friend. In fact, the way it was addressed was odd. It said:

To: Me

From: Me

I pulled the tab and unfolded the note; its contents were short and sweet. Inside a glittery silver box was the blueprint for my future:

Mary Katherine's Life Plan

- become an astronaut
- marry Devon Sawa
- have 3 children (Matt, Addie, and Tinsley)
- buy a farm with Arabian horses
- retire in Disney World

At the ripe age of twelve, my path to happiness was boiled down to a bullet-point list. Bless my little sixth-grade heart, I believed it'd all come true. Mary Katherine Sawa: astronaut, equestrian, and farm-owning mother of three. Somehow, I managed to muck it all up. I wonder what middle school me would say. I imagine she'd be so disappointed.

Where did everything go wrong? We don't have Arabian horses. We are thirty-eight and not even retired. What happened to our plans?

Honestly, I don't know how I'd answer her questions. The truth is—our plans just kept changing. I fell out of love with Devon Sawa and fell in love with Gavin Rossdale. I fell out of love with Gavin and fell in love with Heath Ledger. I lost interest in going to the moon; I wanted to join the FBI. Even now, the list continues to evolve. My ideal life, my road map to happiness, is a target that keeps on moving.

Congresswoman. Biscuit Truck Owner. What I need is a little more money. Okay, money isn't doing it—what I need is a bit of rest. Add "beach vacation" to the list. And since I'll be wearing a bathing suit, and currently feel like a marshmallow, let's add a weight loss goal to the list. That sure adds an element of fun!

I lose five pounds; I gain fifteen. The Biscuit Truck is a bust. The vacation was awesome until it was over. Happiness comes, then it slips out of my grasp. The high of happiness remains short-lived, but it's enough to keep me in pursuit.

• • • • • • •

When I was five years old, Santa Claus delivered the most epic present to my family. It was the last present my siblings and I opened, and we were beyond ecstatic. Poor Teddy Ruxpin and the Cabbage Patch Kids. They just couldn't compete with Nintendo. I was wide-eyed enraptured when my older sister finally gave me a turn. Placing the gray plastic gun in my hand she pointed to the screen and coached me.

It was my first official foray into hunting moving targets.

"Don't worry—it's easy, sis! Just point and shoot all the ducks!"

The ducks started flying, and at first, I did fine. I just kept shooting and shooting at the screen. But then the ducks started flying faster. More and more filled up the screen. Panicked, I fired at everything that moved. But there were just too many targets. In less than a minute, the game was over. I ran to my room and cried.

• • • • • • •

In second grade, I never considered the specific phrasing of that key passage in the Declaration of Independence. But at thirty-eight, and as an author by trade—I believe Thomas Jefferson was letting us in on a secret. Life, we have been given. Liberty, we are owed. But happiness is something else entirely. It's just beyond reach, something to capture. The *pursuit* is all we are promised.

The Declaration of Independence states that humans have certain inherent rights. Rights that are given to us by our Creator, and that governments are created to protect. For generation after generation, elementary schools all over America have prepared adorable Fourth of July programs. Children of every shape and color line up on their lunchroom stage. They sing patriotic songs, wave tiny flags, and wear hilarious gray wigs. And at the end of the play, a couple of students (the teachers' pets) step up to the microphone stands. They smile their little snaggletoothed grins and lead the class in saying:

We hold these truths to be self-evident, that all men are created equal, that they are endowed by their Creator with certain unalienable Rights, that among these are Life, Liberty and the pursuit of Happiness.

And y'all, do we freaking pursue it in the good ole USA. Happiness is the ultimate finish line. Happiness is the American dream. We lace up our shoes, hit the ground running, and cover as much pavement as we can. After all, we have bullet points to knock off our lists! We go for the degree, and we hustle for a house—a place to start the family. To have 2.5 kids, a picket fence, and a dog. A family portrait on the fireplace mantel. We cross our finish lines; we celebrate our wins. We accomplish what we set out to achieve. Then the most confusing thing happens. It's happened to every adult that I know.

There we are, examining the fruits of our labor, an incredible cornucopia of blessings. But even as the medal hangs fresh round our neck, the runner's high starts to wear off.

I'm going to ask you a question, friend. Don't think. Just answer it honestly.

What is the *one thing* you want right now, more than anything else in the world? The thing that would make you feel happy.

Okay, now hold that thought.

Is it a new kitchen? A vacation? To be "high school skinny"? A job change? A new house? A goldendoodle puppy? Some days, if you're like me, it could simply be queso! That's fine. We're being honest right now. Let's keep that energy going.

If I had asked you this same question ten, twenty, thirty years ago…would the answer have been totally different?

Well, obviously, MK. We are grown-ups, now. We aren't pining for a new Teddy Ruxpin.

Bingo! That's what I'm getting at here. We are constantly growing and finding new toys. Happiness is a moving target. It's an emotion dependent on so many variables; it comes and goes with the wind. What made your heart smile yesterday isn't what your heart longs for today.

So, hearts are fickle, and happiness is fleeting, and we'll forever be discontent? Wow. That's really encouraging, MK. So glad I picked up this book.

Okay, I promise that's not where I'm going. Remember how much I love being manic? Feeling happy is one hundred percent my jam. When Dr. C asked, "But at what cost?"—the question was already answered. "The next big thing" is what keeps me going. My dreams make life worthwhile. I will run myself ragged for a Happiness High.

I wonder if you feel the same way.

Here's the thing: You don't have to be bipolar like me to understand the nature of this struggle. We've all experienced this crash in some way or another. It's part of the human experience. But what if I told you we could break this cycle? That we could bypass the frustration. That there's a solution to the perpetual itch in our hearts that keeps us longing for more?

> Happiness is a moving target. It's an emotion dependent on so many variables; it comes and goes with the wind. What made your heart smile yesterday isn't what your heart longs for today.

The late and great comedian Mitch Hedberg once said, "I am sick of following my dreams. I'm just gonna ask them where they're going and hook up with them later."

Mitch was beloved because he understood something: The truth is the funniest joke of all. The truth is we're all tired from running, but I think we are also scared. Scared of what happens if we stop chasing dreams. What if we stop this pursuit of happiness?

Think about it a minute: What would happen if *you* stopped chasing the thing that has made happiness something *out there*, rather than right here? What would that even look like?

· · · · · · ·

Seems like it would be very weird to do a study on happiness in the middle of the Great Depression, but a gaggle of undaunted scientists decided to do just that. The year was 1938, and these researchers took on what would turn out to be a seventy-five-year project, hoping to discover what makes people truly happy. The study began with 268 Harvard students and was broadened to include 465 individuals who lived in the inner-city areas of Boston, Massachusetts.

Health information; career arcs; relationships with spouses, children, extended family, friends—all of it was collected on the subjects. Initially, researchers had theorized that those people with the best educational and financial situations would be those who would report to have the happiest lives. Additionally, things like physiology, intellect, and valued personality traits were also assumed to add to the happiness equation.

So imagine the surprise of researchers when, after compiling data and information for three-quarters of a century, they learned that their presuppositions about the happiness recipe of a great degree, hot body, winning personality, fat bank account, and super brain didn't make for the perfect happiness casserole. "When the study began, nobody cared about empathy or attachment," said psychiatrist George Vaillant, a researcher on the team for almost forty years. But, as it turns out, those were the key factors in what we all search for in the happiness game: The study ultimately revealed that those who lead the happiest lives are those who love others well.

Turns out, the American dream wasn't the promise we thought it might be. In fact, the amount of money or wealth or possessions weighed very little in the outcome. The joyful life doesn't necessarily look like sunshine and roses, Ivy Leagues, and historic homes. We don't have to steeplechase our entire lives; there's a better, simpler way to live, and we're gonna find it together. We'll examine what we know about happiness and peel it apart like an onion. We will take what society says about fulfillment and flip it all upside down. We'll shake out those thoughts and societal standards like a pair of shorts from the dryer—and together we'll discover some shiny new coins of wisdom.

You and I are about to embark on a countercultural, off-road adventure. There's no telling where this journey may lead, so I recommend you pack lightly. Maybe, for a while, let go of your dreams—your visions of how life should be. Don't worry, you can always hook up with them later—if that's something you still want to do.

What I want, and what I think you are looking for, is some meaning in the mundane. To have fulfillment in our daily lives and contentment in our homes. There is a different kind of wealth that exists for the person who discovers they simply need less. It's a richness—not of a bank account—but of the heart and soul. It is found in our interactions with friends and family, in the jobs we are already working. It's out there, y'all: the joy we've been craving. It's more of a choice than a chase. But first we have to set aside our plans…turn off Google Maps for a while. This is the ride where you roll down the windows and let your hand fly out in the wind. Enough with the finish lines; they're always moving.

Let's go find some joy in the journey.

CHAPTER 1

IN THE WEEDS

He who hunts for flowers will find flowers.
He who loves weeds will find weeds.
—Henry Ward Beecher

I remember sitting in an understuffed chair, waiting for the counselor to arrive. The office decor had a split personality. There was no obvious vibe to the place. The floral lampshade said, "Let's have a spot of tea," but the artwork was throwing me off—a concert poster for Widespread Panic and a circle of Grateful Dead bears. Our counselor was either an old British woman or a middle-aged pothead hipster.

Ian's hand was cold and clammy; he was probably having a panic attack. Neither of us was particularly looking forward to premarital counseling, but it was required to be married in the church. Still, we were young and poor, and counseling wasn't cheap. So when I found a place that offered income-based payments, I booked the first available appointment. There was chatter down the hall; the counselor was back from lunch. I checked the time. Twenty minutes late. Pothead hipster, I decided.

The door opened, and in walked our premarital counselors. Not one, but two. A couple. The woman had wild strawberry hair, and she was wearing a Grateful Dead T-shirt. I noticed a skunky smell in the room.

"I'm Hannah! And this is my husband, Pete. Welcome to LoveWell ministries. Do you mind if I ask where you found us?"

"Google," I responded.

"Good ole Google!" Pete declared. "Well, we are glad you are here. Before we get started, a little about us. Hannah and I started LoveWell ministries when we got married last year. She was a realtor, and I was a car salesman, and we'd both had bad luck with marriage."

"Oh," I said. I couldn't hide my surprise. "So you've only been married a year?"

Hannah reached over and grabbed Pete's hand. "One glorious, love-filled year."

I could feel Ian's eyeballs burning a hole in my cheek. He was gonna give me so much hell for this. Of course I would book our premarital counseling with two stoned newlyweds who had several divorces between them, and not a single credential to speak of.

Thirty minutes later, we peeled out of that parking lot,

laughing so hard we were crying. We were thirty dollars poorer and had learned absolutely nothing about marriage. But we'd checked off the box of premarital counseling. First Baptist would let us get married. Our permission slip was officially validated by the stoners at LoveWell ministries.

Fast-forward to a few months later, and the Backstroms were on our honeymoon. We decided to stop in Savannah for the night before heading to Hilton Head Island. Ian had heard there was an epic ghost tour, and he had a thing for anything haunted. The trolley ride was indeed epic, but not in the way we had planned. A few minutes before the tour began, we had a massive fight. Something about dinner, or directions, or who the heck knows. I can't remember the details.

What I do remember is staring out the window, my ears tuning in and out, as our tour guide animatedly described every haunted nook and cranny of that beautiful city.

So there I was, marinating in anger over some trivial fight, listening to Alex the Tour Guide, wondering whether Ian and I would haunt the same building or separate ones after we murdered each other.

I was pulled back to reality by Alex recounting the story of yet another haunting. This time, the ghost was a cat. I imagined a world in which Ghost Ian divorced me, and I became another stop on the tour. The Undead Cat Lady...such a beautiful bride, but her honeymoon ended so badly.

The truth is, having a seasoned tour guide made the night a memorable experience. Despite the fact that both Ian and I were wearing our grumpy pants that evening, we both remember multiple stories from the haunted trolley experience. Alex had traveled those roads a thousand times, and it showed in his expertise. He was so animated, so deeply familiar with those moonlit streets of Savannah…like the city was his one true love.

It occurred to me that what Ian and I needed was our own little version of Alex.

A tour guide to help us navigate those trickier bits of marriage. It could have saved us so much pain, and so many ruined date nights.

• • • • • • •

When I was in my early twenties, I decided to pick up a hitchhiker. Well, technically her thumb wasn't out or anything, so maybe it didn't qualify as hitchhiking. I'm not sure what the rules are for that. But either way, she asked for a ride, and I gave her one, and it was about as sketchy a situation as you could imagine. It all started when I drove to meet Ian for lunch at the hospital in downtown Orlando. He had just started residency and we'd just moved to town, so big-city life was new to me. I hadn't yet learned certain metropolitan skills like locking doors or minding my own business. So, when I was approached by an older lady who needed a ride home, my naive little heart was like, *Yes, MK. Take this sweet lady home. This is what Jesus would want.*

We got in the car, and I asked her to buckle up.

"Nope," she said. "I'm good."

I wasn't sure how to respond to that, but I assumed she had her reasons. Perhaps she had stitches or a broken clavicle. She'd just left the hospital, after all.

"So, where are we going?" I asked my new friend. She broadly gestured to the right. I pulled out of the parking lot and started driving, assuming she'd give instructions when necessary. A few minutes into our little excursion, she reached into a grocery sack and pulled out a can of Mad Dog. She cracked it open and drank like a camel. I was starting to get concerned.

"I'm new here, but I think there's an open container law. Do you mind finishing your drink at home?"

"Nope, I'm good." She finished the drink and crunched the can. Hand to God, y'all, she tossed it on the floorboard.

I decided to be grateful she didn't chuck it out the window. I was starting to worry we might get pulled over.

"Ma'am, do you mind giving me your address? So I know about where we're going?"

"STOP!" she yelled. I just about wrecked turning into the 7-Eleven. I pulled my car into a parking spot and my heart felt heavy. "Ma'am," I said, "do you live here?"

"Nope," she said. "I'm hungry."

But she didn't get out. She just sat and waited.

"Um…" I wasn't sure what to do. "Would…you like me to get you a snack?"

"Yep."

I grabbed my purse and went inside, leaving the car on for... *What is her name?* Perusing the snack aisle, I could feel a panic attack setting in. What should I do? I didn't know the answer. I decided to phone a friend.

Scrolling through my contacts, I could play out exactly how each of these calls would unfold.

Mom: "You did what?"

Dad: "You picked up who?"

Sis: "MK, I swear to God."

I needed my husband, but I knew not to call when he was on shift unless it was an emergency. I wasn't sure this was an emergency...but I wasn't sure that it wasn't. I peeked outside, and my car was still there, but it looked like she'd opened another can of Mad Dog.

I sighed and dialed Ian's number.

"Hey, babe, I'm busy. Everything okay?"

"Uh," I replied. "I'm not sure?"

"What do you mean?" he asked, sounding concerned. I could hear machines beeping in the background.

"Okay, don't be mad, but...I picked up this lady. She asked for a ride home and..."

"MK, no."

"Well, she's not being mean or anything like that. But she isn't listening to me, either. She keeps opening beers and she won't buckle up. I don't think she knows where she lives."

For a moment, there was only silence on his end. I just knew he was pinching the bridge of his nose.

"MK where are you?" he asked with tension in his voice.

"I'm at a 7-Eleven, buying her snacks," I replied. And as it left my mouth, I knew how stupid it sounded.

"Okay," Ian said, taking a deep breath. "Here's what you're going to do."

I didn't have a plan of my own, so I followed Ian's instructions. I bought Doritos and a coke, requested twenty dollars cash, then went outside to my car. It was still there, and my friend was, too. I walked over to the passenger side. I opened the door, and two empty cans of Mad Dog fell out into the parking lot.

"Ma'am, I'm really sorry about this—but I need to get home. I've got some Doritos and a little bit of cash. Do you think you can find a different ride?"

"Yep," she said, climbing out of my car, unfazed by this sudden change of plans. She shoved the chips and the money in her grocery sack, and that was it. She just walked away.

I got back in my car and buckled my seat belt.

What in the world just happened?

• • • • • • •

Have you ever had a full circle moment?

It's like déjà vu, but not exactly, because the sensation is not imagined. Full-circle moments are like watching a movie reboot, but with a moment from your very own life. It feels strangely familiar except instead of wondering if you've been here before, you *know* you have. You recognize exactly what is happening, but some of the details are slightly different.

Last spring, my family relocated back to Alabama after nearly a decade away. I now have the privilege of watching my children experience the world I grew up in. I've been able to see some of the happier memories from my own childhood through their eyes and encounter what brought me joy decades ago from a fresh angle.

Not long after we moved, plenty of boxes still taped shut and stacked in corners, my daughter, Holland, brought me a purple handpicked bouquet. The memory associated with those tiny flowers came flooding back with such a force that I had to catch my breath.

> Full-circle moments are like watching a movie reboot, but with a moment from your very own life.

In an instant, it was 1989, and I was walking home from school, curating a bouquet of the oddest little purple flowers to give to my mother. I called the flowers "Fraggle Rock Flowers" because the buds reminded me of a Fraggle. (Remember that show with the underground Muppets and the upbeat, catchy theme song?)

Every day, I would collect my Fraggle Rock Flowers and hand them to my momma. It was a gesture of love, a sign that I thought of her as I made my way home.

Momma always received this offering with an exclamation of "How beautiful!" I would tip my head with pride, my good-daughter vibe renewed each afternoon.

Something you need to know about my momma: She is an expert gardener. That woman doesn't just have green thumbs, she's practically the Hulk. The woman can *grow* some flowers. Like, the ones that are hard to grow. Lilies. Roses. Irises. Spectacular blossoms with romantic names like "Heirloom Heart's Blood" and "Heritage Cream." If these flowers were people, they would live on a golf course and drive Lexus SUVs.

And because my momma is a fancy flower lady, she knew something that I didn't. Those purple little fraggles that I loved so much? They were commonly known as henbit. Yes, henbit. I can't even with that name, it is so weird. It sounds like a cat toy made of feathers or some form of digital currency.

You might ask: What kind of person would come up with a name as horribly drab as henbit? The same kind of person that would classify this precious plant as a weed.

The day I learned this devastating information was the day I stopped making bouquets. Momma knew something was wrong that day when I came home empty-handed.

"No Fraggle Rock Flowers today?" she asked with a smile.

"They aren't even flowers, Mom," I responded with a

frown. "I picked some on the playground today, and the teacher said they were weeds."

Well, Momma was having none of that. She sat down at the table right then and there, and gave me an education in botany. This is what I learned:

Turns out, flowers are finicky things that require very specific soil and conditions and light and hydration in order to survive. But weeds, like my little Fraggle Rock friends, are more like dainty little warriors. They survive in less-than-ideal conditions. They can grow in the sidewalk cracks, in acidic soil, or in places where water is scarce.

While an iris, for example, needs someone like my momma to tend to its every fancy, henbits pop up and bloom and spread of their own accord. No wonder Fraggle Rock Flowers make my heart smile. They have a resilience, a strong construction, that sets them apart from the flowers. They're tiny little mascots of joy.

Whereas happiness is more like the beautiful iris, entirely dependent on the right conditions. Not enough attention from your spouse and you start to wilt. Bad day at work, and you're dropping blooms and turning a sick shade of yellow. Happiness is fickle and flaky and fleeting…

But joy, on the other hand? It's got that wild weed constitution. It blooms wherever it's planted. Joy takes the rain as it comes, and slurps it up with a smile. It will spring up in the cracks of all kinds of chaos in your life. Joy knows how to flourish in situations that would take down a hothouse flower.

Joy doesn't always make that much sense, and sometimes we confuse its blooms with the flowers of happiness in life. But when we start to understand what joy can endure and what it can do, compared with its flightier sister, well…that's when joy shows its deepest definition.

I love that my momma showed me how to appreciate different kinds of flora. How to curate happiness's fragile petals, how to cherish joy's hardy stalks. How there's beauty in both bouquets.

There's nothing wrong with gathering happiness whenever and wherever you can; happiness is a bright and beautiful thing. But what I do want to do is encourage you to seek a different kind of harvest, one that's found in the chaotic wild, one that springs up in the cracks and crevices of life. What you and I are going to find is this feisty little thing called joy.

But before we do, let's make one thing clear: This isn't LoveWell ministries. I'll be danged if a single reader finishes this book and feels duped by my lack of credentials. My disclosure is posted on the door. There are no experts on this journey to joy, only fellow travelers. We've all been dreaming of the same destination and gotten a little lost on the way. So, if we want to find joy in this ride

> Fraggle Rock Flowers make my heart smile. They have a resilience, a strong construction, that sets them apart from the flowers. They're tiny little mascots of joy.

of our life, we have to start living with intention. We have to map out a plan and get in the driver's seat, and study the rules of the road.

I used to be a hitchhiker on the road to joy; I was a passenger in my own life. I'd let anything pick me up and carry me along, just hoping I'd land somewhere good. But the thing is, consigning your joy journey and taking the passenger seat is a terrible plan indeed. God knows what parking lot you might end up in, waiting for the next car to come.

So here's what I'm offering, friends. Allow me to be your Alex. Join me in this journey to joy, even for just a short while. There are so many stories I'm excited to tell you, so many nuggets of truth.

I won't claim to be any sort of expert, but what I am is a well-seasoned traveler. Joy is my passion, my hope, and my purpose. Like Alex, I know these parts well. I've been on this journey for a good while now, and I've learned a few things along the way.

Allow me to point out the pops of color in your life that you might not have noticed. Allow me to point out those hearty little henbits blooming through cracks in the sidewalks.

I'm still learning the ways of joy. I'm still taking this journey. I can't promise you that I've got it all figured out, but what I can do is promise you this: You and I are going to laugh together. We're going to figure this out. We are going to think a little bit, drink some coffee, then think a little bit more. We're going to reevaluate what we're searching for and strip away every barrier. And when Fraggle Rock Flowers come blooming through the cracks, we are going to make a bouquet. Because the beauty of joy isn't found in a garden. It doesn't grow in neat little rows. It's found in the crevices, the cracks, and the chaos.

Like flowers…but a little more wild.

> The beauty of joy isn't found in a garden. It doesn't grow in neat little rows. It's found in the crevices, the cracks, and the chaos.

. . . .

TOUR GUIDE TAKEAWAYS

- How you define joy has a lot to do with how you pursue it. And the way we develop our definitions of joy is a whole mixed pantry of things: what our parents told us would bring us joy; how our faith systems defined it; and our own personal experiences with elation, fulfillment, happiness, achievement, and romance. How do you define joy? And how has that definition been working for you?

- How do you think you've been making the joy journey to this point? Have you been a hitchhiker, along for the ride, assuming circumstances and situations have the wheel and will get you where you want to go? Or have you been following supposed "experts," who promise the perfect business plan or strategy or approach to bring you the ultimate in joyful fulfillment? What do you think might happen if you become responsible for your joy? What needs to change to move you to that position?

- Do you think joy and happiness are the same? Or are they different?

. . . .

CHAPTER 2

JOY IS A FORCE

For every action, there is an equal
and opposite reaction.
—Sir Isaac Newton's third law of motion

Confession time (and this one is weird): I have a crush on Sir Isaac Newton. I know, I know. It could never happen. He's a genius physicist, I failed Math 098. He's dead, and I'm alive. Maybe it's a star-crossed lovers thing. Whatever it is, I adore him. You can keep Sheldon from *The Big Bang Theory*; Sir Ike is mine. He's the guy who, back in the late 1600s and early 1700s, figured out all kinds of things about gravity and put together the laws of motion. He developed calculus. He was a theologian and a philosopher. He developed color theory and figured out which comets were hurtling toward earth and which ones weren't. And while this isn't specifically mentioned in literature, I feel like he could make an exquisite omelet.

And I realize this next statement may be a little controversial, but I stand by it: He was sort of attractive too. In a flowing-white-wig, severe-intense-stare, eighteenth-century kind of way. It's hard to explain, but a man in a waistcoat and breeches just awakens something inside of me. *Outlander* changed me as a woman, and I know a relic hottie when I see one. Sir Isaac is giving serious Jamie Frasier vibes. He's a babe, and I dare you to fight me on this.

But brilliant achievements and breeches aside, there's a bigger reason for my slight fixation on this long-dead, famous physicist. And it has everything to do with forces and light and art and Newtonian law. And puppy love. And college breakups. And an unexpected lesson in joy.

• • • • • • •

My first love was a sixth-grade skater boy named Jamie. Some might say it was "puppy love," but what does that mean to a puppy? The feelings I had were as big as they were real, and you couldn't tell my twelve-year-old heart otherwise. Jamie declared it was "love at first sight," which is honest-to-God hilarious, considering how we met. As with any great romance, backstory matters. Let's take a quick trip back in time.

My very first day at Girard Middle School, I unknowingly made an enemy. And not just any run-of-the-mill enemy, because that would be too easy. I'd managed to piss off the seventh-grade Queen of Mean, Christie Sharpe. She was like

Regina George, but going through puberty, an absolute freaking delight.

I'd spoken with Christie once in my life, in the cafeteria on the first day of school. I was scanning the lunchroom for an empty seat when my eyes found a familiar face: Trini, the yellow Power Ranger, my childhood hero and muse. Unable to contain my excitement, I trotted right over to Christie's table.

"I love your Power Ranger lunch box!" I squealed, striking my very best ninja pose. Christie stopped mid-chew and glared. Her minions exchanged nervous glances, but nobody said a word. Now, a socially savvy kid would have known what to do in the face of that cold, dark silence: shut up, tuck tail, and run.

But no. Not I. Not me.

No one has ever accused me of being socially savvy, and that is *not* what I did.

"Sabertooth tiger griffon thunderzord power!" I yelled while punching and kicking the air. If these girls loved Power Rangers, even a little, they would be blown away at my skills.

Turns out, the girls weren't Power Rangers fans. Not even a little bit. Christie was only carrying Trini because she'd lost her Lisa Frank lunch box. She was already a little self-conscious about this Power Rangers lunchtime accessory and I, naively and unintentionally, made her feel downright humiliated. I was awkward and lonely and looking to make friends.

But a collection of enemies is what I got.

In response to my Power Rangers callout, Christie and her

cronies took to teaching me the consequences of violating the Embarrassing Lunch Box protocol. With lookouts posted to divert any lunchroom teachers' aides, they hustled me out of the cafeteria and to a quiet area where we could, um, discuss my faux pax. The conversation was short, the action decisive. I found myself shoved into the trash, Screech Powers–style, by a posse of revenge-seeking seventh graders.

Those girls were surprisingly strong, come to think of it. They executed their mission and left me, stuck by the butt, in the science hall trash can.

And that's the moment I met Jamie. He was wandering down the hall, minding his own business, when what did he see but me, helpless as a flipped-over June bug, folded into a nasty trash can, shins and shoulders dangling. He dug me out, helped me clean up, and walked me to gym, chatting all the way there.

After that, we just never stopped talking.

Each day at recess we'd share a Mountain Dew. Jamie was kind and he made me laugh, and my heart went pitter-pat. We sat next to each other and passed notes during science— until the day we got caught. That was the first time (and not the last) we would wind up in the principal's office. Momma was livid, but I didn't mind. It was thrilling to be in trouble with Jamie. We were our own nerdy version of Bonnie and Clyde, note-passing laws be damned.

• • • • • • •

The week before winter break, Jamie asked me to a movie. Technically, I wasn't allowed to date until I was old enough to drive, but my negotiating skills were strong, and I was able to strike a deal with Momma: I could go to the early-bird senior-discount showing…with a cousin chaperone. A little awkward, but at that age what isn't? My first date was in the books!

That Saturday, my stomach was in knots. My big sister hot-rolled my hair. My killer outfit was laid out on my bed, brown stirrup pants and a brown ribbed turtleneck, too. Jamie said that brown was my color, and I was leaning hard into that statement. I got dressed, but still felt a little chilly, so I grabbed my favorite sweatshirt. It was ice blue, adorned with an intricate snow scene involving teddy bears on skis. I pulled it on over my brown turtleneck and stood in front of the mirror.

Yes, I thought. *This looks great. A perfect outfit for my very first date.*

• • • • • • •

The movie was terrible. Half a star would be generous. Some bad guys in Jersey blew up a tunnel with a whole bunch of people inside. There was toxic waste, explosions, bad guys, and pretty much everyone died. Except Sylvester Stallone, who, for some odd reason, was perfectly prepared for this scenario. In his moment of triumph, Stallone held an actual bomb in his fist and yelled to the bad guys, "I have found your heart, and I'm gonna blow it right out of you!"

Then everything went *kapow*.

I looked at Jamie, expecting a laugh, but instead he leaned over and kissed me.

Unexpected. Thrilled. I was ready to accept his proposal and move on to naming our children.

Monday at recess, Jamie bought Mountain Dew…but he didn't offer to share it. In gym class he played with an all-boys team, so I sat in the bleachers with friends. When school let out for winter break, Jamie didn't say goodbye. It stung a little, but I tried to understand. After all, he had *kissed* me. I chalked it up to his upcoming winter break trip. Both of us were kids of divorce and we bonded over the experience of packing up on a regular basis to go visit parents. Jamie's situation was further complicated by how far away his father lived. He was scheduled to spend the holidays with his dad, a long trip and lots of miles from home. I figured he was sad to leave town.

I counted the days until winter break was over and I would see Jamie again at school. The first day back, I got to school early. I couldn't wait to see him. I had another new brown shirt, and so much to tell him, and I knew he'd be thrilled to see me. I smiled when I saw his brother's car pull up with Jamie in the passenger seat to drop-off, but the flutter of my heart was short-lived.

There was a girl on the sidewalk, lingering, and when

Jamie hopped out of the car, he hugged *her*. Not me. Not the girl who had been waiting all of winter break for him to return. Who in the heck was—*Lacy?!*

I felt my stomach turning over. Lacy, one of Christie's mean-girl minions. One of the girls who pushed me into the trash can. Surely, Jamie knew? I felt stupid for wearing this brown shirt. I ran to the bathroom and hid in a stall, trying to process what happened.

What was Jamie doing? Was he trying to hurt me? In a million years, I wouldn't understand. He'd kicked me aside like a crunched-up Mountain Dew can…for a bully in fancy jeans. The warning bell rang; I stayed put. I could not, would not, go to my new homeroom class looking a hot dang mess. I soaked a paper towel in cool water and dabbed my face in front of the mirror, hoping the little red splotches would fade away quickly.

Get it together, I thought to myself. *He's just a stupid boy. A stupid boy who squeaks when he talks. Who kisses like a hungry giraffe.*

I felt some coolness return to my cheeks. Anger was oddly comforting. It seemed the polar opposite of the hurt I was experiencing—but every bit as powerful.

"I. Hate. Jamie. Pratt." The words came out with venom, and I was surprised how honest they felt. Suddenly, I felt less fragile. It was like my anger filled the room and sadness had nowhere to sit. What was it we were just learning in science? That Sir Isaac Newton stuff? *Forces come in pairs.*

That was it. The solution to my problem: Anger was a force that fought away sadness. Anger could be my superpower. It was my spider bite gone wrong. My villain origin story. No more butterflies in my stomach, just red-eyed screeching bats. I'd burn my feelings for Jamie to the ground and salt the scorched earth left in my wake. I would squash the feelings I had for him with a force that was equal and opposite.

I didn't have to cry over Jamie. I'd choose to hate him, instead.

• • • • • • •

Six years later, it was my freshman year of college and my life was an absolute train wreck. My grades were skid marks on the tracks. The university put me on academic probation after my first semester. The upcoming semester was my last chance to turn that ship around. All I needed was a 2.5, which I realize sounds quite reasonable—but my GPA was so low it couldn't buy a McChicken. The mountain before me was steep.

My strategy was to take a bunch of electives for spring semester: drama, public speaking, and art. How hard could it be to act, talk, and paint? I was betting with pretty good odds. The first day back after Christmas break, I had theater and public speaking—and my plan was rolling out beautifully. I had a flair for drama and could talk to a post, and both professors were thrilled to have me. I had no worry that art would be different. My crayons and markers were ready.

On Tuesday, my art professor burst into class, rolling a giant projector. Her skirt was flowy, her hair was wild, and she was slurping a giant iced coffee. She reminded me of Ms. Frizzle, of *Magic School Bus* fame.

"To understand color," the professor chirped, "you first must understand light!"

She flipped a switch on the projector and an illustration appeared on-screen: Anatomy of the Human Eye. I peeked at my syllabus to make sure I was in the right class. Yep. Theory of Color.

I'd expected to paint some happy little trees, not label the sclera of an eyeball. I prayed this class would make a quick turn, back in a Bob Ross direction.

"Ma'am? You. Right there, third row." The professor was pointing to me.

"Yes?" I squirmed in my seat.

"What are the three primary colors?" she asked.

"Red, yellow, and blue?" I asked.

She didn't tell me if I was right or wrong; she only turned to address the class.

"Ladies and gentlemen, everything you know about color is wrong. Perhaps you've heard of Isaac Newton," Professor Frizzle said. She reached into her pocket and pulled out a beautiful crystal. "He was working with a prism just like this, when he noticed something remarkable."

The professor held her crystal up and a prism of light appeared on the wall. She beamed with satisfaction and continued, "He discovered that sunlight isn't actually white, but the combination of each color. These additive qualities led Newton to believe there were mathematical relationships between colors. He inspected the prism and noticed that violet and red were both very similar—so he bent the band into a hoop, creating the first color circle. That's when mathematical relationships between color were first realized."

Professor Frizzle moved the prism of color around the classroom. A few athletes in the very back row jumped up and pretended to catch it like overzealous kittens.

"Isaac Newton created color theory," Professor Frizzle declared. "Everybody say, 'Thank you, Isaac!'"

The class was too cool to respond.

• • • • • • •

A few weeks into spring semester, I found myself crying in a frat house bathroom, my breath smelling like cheap vodka. Six years after my first breakup with Jamie, my luck with love hadn't improved.

My next ex-boyfriend, Tyler, was in the house with some other girl. Based on the lack of surprise in the crowd, I was the only one who hadn't seen it coming. They were an item, and I was an idiot, and I wanted to disappear.

My friend Lindsey wiped away my mascara and handed me a cup of water. "MK, we need to get you home. If Tyler

goes home with that skank in a glitter belt, he's stupider than
he looks."

"I hate Tyler!" I said, sipping at the water. "I hate him, and
I hate her, too." Superpower activated.

"Good," she said. "Now dry up your eyes. We're going to
Taco Bell."

· · · · · · ·

After the frat house breakup, I stopped showing up to class.
Drama, public speaking, and Ms. Frizzle be hanged. I guess
it felt better to fail by absence than to show up and find out I
was stupid. It came as no surprise when summer rolled around
and my college broke up with me, too. The letter I received
was the academic equivalent of "We just need some space."
After a year, I could return when I'd (assumingly) become
more mature.

I embarked on some serious soul-searching that year, in
a journey circling the globe. I waitressed at Chili's in Dallas,
Texas. I volunteered as a teacher in Thailand. I went vegan,
and failed, so I went vegetarian (an endeavor that ended with
bacon).

One year later, I was one year older, with a lot more
questions than answers. But probation was over, and I was
welcomed back to campus. Plus, I had nothing better to do.
So, I registered for classes, and packed my things.

Freshman year, take two.

I moved into my dorm the Saturday before classes resumed and a little after midnight my phone buzzed. I recognized the number, and my stomach dropped. My ex. He knew I was back.

"Hello?" I answered, trying to sound cool.

"MK?" He sounded surprised.

"It's me. My number hasn't changed."

The silence between us lingered, and dammit, I knew better than this, to stay on a silent phone line, pathetically waiting.

"Look," I said, preparing to hang up. "If you're calling to—"

"I'm calling to apologize. MK, you are a good person. And...I treated you so bad. You didn't deserve that. Nobody does. I just wanted to say I'm sorry."

"You are...apologizing? To me?"

"Yes."

Well, that was completely off my radar.

The strangest thing happened when he spoke those words. I felt like the Grinch who stole Christmas. No, not the scene where he grins an evil grin. The one where his heart grows bigger. I didn't need to hate Tyler anymore, and it turned out: That was a relief. The anger I carried inside my heart was as harmful as the breakup itself.

"I forgive you," I said, and it felt so good. We hung up the call with kindness. It wasn't your typical happy ending; I never spoke to Tyler again. But there is peace in my heart where hate once resided. There is joy where there was once resentment. We both moved on to happier lives, and I know in my heart that's a win.

· · · · · · ·

What does all this have to do with my personal Sir Isaac Newton fan club? Well, let me tell you. Sir Isaac Newton was all about understanding forces. Not that I claim to be some seasoned guide on him, but when I swirl his genius on some topics into the palette of my crazy life, I find some profound truth there.

Let's start with his theories on forces. He's the guy who came up with the laws of motion, and it's the third law of motion that says that for every action there's an equal and opposite reaction, that the force of the first action is met by an opposite and same-size action on the other side.

Here's where I got it wrong.

In my heartbreaks, those of the middle school and college kind and beyond, those that populate your world and mine in breath-stealing and joy-crushing ways, I often applied what I

> There is joy where there was once resentment. We both moved on to happier lives, and I know in my heart that's a win.

thought I knew of Newton's third law. *You wanna hurt me? Fine. I'm going to get madder than an old wet hen.* (And if you don't speak Southern, you should know that it doesn't get madder than soaked specimens of the poultry sort.) That was my solution. *I'll throw some nasty words about you up on a bathroom wall as a monument to the ways you wronged me.* That was my way of trying to come back to a place of joy, that place I thought I was before I got hurt. That was my third law of relational dynamics. That was my action against the actions of loss, pain, betrayal, and abandonment.

I just figured anger was the opposite of hurt, the force that sat on the other side of the equation. And I thought it would somehow boomerang me back to a place of joy, or at least some place other than the Taco Bell drive-thru window.

And that's where Sir Isaac Newton's work on color theory comes in.

(If you're a science teacher, here's where you might need to walk away and come back in a bit because I'm likely going to butcher all pure Newtonian theory here with a dull knife and it's not gonna look pretty. But it's what it looks like in my head and heart.)

See, Sir Ike also had a lot to say about color, and I credit my brief tenure in Professor Frizzle's college art class for helping introduce me to this part of his work. Sir Isaac Newton observed that when he used that prism of his to split white light, seven colors would result, "ROY G BIV" (red, orange, yellow, green, blue, indigo, and violet). He then organized what he was discovering about color onto a color wheel, to show those shades that were opposite from each other and those that were closely related. I would have told you that blue was the opposite of red. I would have told you purple is the opposite of orange.

Just like I would have told you that the opposite of hurt is anger and hate and that sadness is the opposite of joy. I would have told you that joy is the opposite of anything that goes wrong, doesn't feel good, doesn't meet my expectations, doesn't work out the way I want.

But when you see color laid out on the color wheel, you discover that what you thought would be opposites aren't. Green is the opposite of red, not blue. Orange is the opposite of blue, not purple. Yellow is the opposite of violet.

Stay with me. Here's where I attempt to wrap up my combined MK's Theory of Forces and Color as They Pertain to Joy.

When you and I are trying to make our way

> I just figured anger was the opposite of hurt, the force that sat on the other side of the equation. And I thought it would somehow boomerang me back to a place of joy, or at least some place other than the Taco Bell drive-thru window.

to joy, whether we're trying to go back to a place where we think we experienced it or whether we're recognizing that maybe we've never really known or understood joy, we may be hanging on to things that are the opposite of joy and prevent us from going there. Or we may snuggle up next to things that we think are close to joy, thinking we're at least getting in the vicinity, but we actually are all the way across the board from where we really want to go.

And those forces that create the push and pull in our hearts, those actions that we think will take us one place but dump us in another, that's where we need help. We need to recalibrate our actions and our perceptions about the force and light that is joy.

We've got to stop fighting against it and make our way toward it. We've got to stop getting in our own way.

What if we embrace the laws of joy dynamics? Those laws usually don't follow what feels intuitive or cultural or expected. Just like Sir Ike's discoveries.

Imagine you can travel back in time and talk to yourself as a child. Not just for a minute, but for a few hours. What kind of things would you say? I think we'd all be tempted to guide our younger selves away from hurtful experiences. *Stay away from that boy; he'll break your heart! Stay away from that friend; she'll hurt you! Stay away from that job; it's an absolute nightmare! Stay away from Aristocrat Vodka!*

But the truth is, part of the human experience is discovering new ways to get hurt. Pain is an unavoidable force—there is no bubble wrap for protecting our hearts. If I could go back to myself as a child, I think that's what I'd tell her. I would hold her hand, scooch up close, and acknowledge the pain in the journey. But then I would smile and tell her a little secret we discovered along the way. The physics of light and color and force—all lessons in growth and healing.

There are seasons in life that are cold and gray, and you'll struggle to remember life's beauty. You might even be tempted to buy into the belief that the world has *lost* its color. Listen to me, that is a lie. I imagine your soul behaves much like a prism. The capacity for beauty never leaves, but there are times you just won't see it. Don't give up on yourself, or your journey. There are curtains all around us to poke holes through. *Get up and go searching for light.*

We've got to stop fighting against joy and make our way toward it. We've got to stop getting in our own way.

And there's something else Isaac Newton taught me. Things like love and peace and joy, they make this life worth living. But there will also be forces like hate, discontent, and despair, all equal and opposite in power, gunning to keep us from the joy that can be ours. My job, your job, is to learn how to fight back with what can push away the darkness, not add to it.

I'm here to tell you: Joy is a profound force. Like, one of the top superpowers. More powerful than anger, mightier than hate. I haven't always understood how to seek it and how to use it, but I'm learning.

I didn't make it right with Professor Frizzle at the time. I know she put her heart and soul into those lectures, and I doubt she knows how much her class, abbreviated as it was for me, has stayed with me. So, in homage to Professor Frizzle and nerdy eighteenth-century philosopher/theologian/ theorists everywhere, let's join our voices together.

Are you ready? Everybody say, "Thank you, Isaac!"

Thank you, Isaac.

· ·

TOUR GUIDE TAKEAWAYS

- Snuggle up real close and tell me: Who was your first crush? How did it turn out? What wild declarations and expectations did you have for that puppy love? Did it fizzle or end in a heartbreak?

- As we talked about, there are opposite forces at work in our lives, powerful emotions that pull us and create tension. Sometimes we want to use what we think is an opposite emotion to cancel out hurt, betrayal, and loss. What are the forces you've tried to use against tough emotions? What do you think would happen if you tried using forgiveness, grace, healthy boundaries, and self-compassion instead?

- Even though I was not a teacher's delight, I still delight in many of the things I learned from my teachers. Who is a teacher you think back on with affection? What did you learn from this teacher? How do you use it today?

· ·

CHAPTER 3

FLOWERS FOR THE DEAD

Who wants flowers when you're dead?
Nobody.

—J. D. Salinger, *The Catcher in the Rye*

The server showed up to my table with a coke and paused, looking for a place to put it.

"I'm sorry," I said, moving a book out of the way. "I have too many things to read."

He said, "I see that," as he was setting down my coke. "The Dalai Lama, *Star Wars*, and…Dr. Seuss?"

"It's weird," I admitted. "But I'm writing a book—and I guess you could call this research?"

"Looks like you have a good start," he said. "But a science journal and *Star Wars*?"

"Well, I'm starting to believe that joy is a force, instead of a bunch of emotions. And I'm curious if it's possible for some people to have a genetic sensitivity to the joy force.

"You know, kinda like—the Jedi!"

He said, "Exactly!"

I couldn't tell if he was excited about *Star Wars* or joy, but he was excited, and that was encouraging.

"So, are you a *Star Wars* fan?" I asked.

"I am," he replied. "But...I have a master's degree in philosophy. So, this is sort of my thing."

I couldn't believe my luck. "That's perfect! Wanna sit down and tell me about it?"

He looked at the books, then around the room, then sighed with obvious disappointment.

"I would love to, but I just got three tables! I have to go take some orders. But since you're reading about joy, can I make a recommendation? You're going to think I am crazy."

"Oh, please." I laughed. "It can't be that bad. What's your recommendation?"

"Nietzsche," he replied, then hurried away to greet his three new tables.

And he was right. I thought he was crazy.

So...I took his advice.

• • • • • • •

The hipster bookseller at Barnes and Noble clicked through a few screens and scrolled. "We have several titles by Friedrich Nietzsche, which one are you looking for?"

I knew only two things about Friedrich Nietzsche. One, that his name was hard to spell. And two, that he fathered nihilism. Technically, nihilism is the rejection of all moral and religious principles, and it promotes the idea that life has no meaning. Nontechnically, I like to think of nihilism as a cranky teenager, giving the the ultimate shoulder shrug and eye roll at the meaning and purpose of human existence. Nihilism throws religious and moral ideas the finger and gives a high-handed laugh while it does so. I had a sense of Nietzsche's depressing view of life, which made the idea that he had something to say about joy even more intriguing.

What I didn't know was a single title he penned. I tried to play it cool.

"They're all so delightful," I replied to the bookseller. "Which books do you have in store?"

The bookseller gave me a curious look. He returned to the list on his screen.

"Uh, let's see. We've got *God Is Dead. The Anti-Christ. Untimely Meditations.*"

"Any of his…lighter work?" I asked sheepishly.

The bookseller cracked a smile. "How about *Thus Spoke Zarathustra?*"

I took the book home, put on some pajamas, and poured a cup of tea. I curled up on the couch and glanced at my strange new friend.

"All right, Mr. Nietzsche," I said to the book. "Let's hear about nihilistic joy."

• • • • • • •

I grew up in a Southern family that loved to visit dead relatives. We had a family plot at Maple Hill, a beautiful cemetery that was scattered with colorful maple trees and enclosed with a two-hundred-year-old stone wall. I remember there being a playground, too, which in retrospect seems quite strange. But because this was a cultural norm in my family, I've always been comfy in graveyards. Perhaps even a little too comfortable.

Growing up in the '80s, half my childhood was spent wandering around, unsupervised, with neighborhood friends. My best friend, Lauren, lived four doors down and right across the street from Maple Hill. Every weekend, we'd climb the old stone wall and frolic around the cemetery. We'd read the old gravestones, collect colorful leaves, and create worlds of magical adventure. But all our fun came to a cold, hard stop the day we decided to host a luau in Lauren's den. We invited our parents to the Hawaiian celebration, which included entertainment and dinner. We built a menu from pantry items, like

Hawaiian sweet rolls and canned pineapple. We found a cassette tape of Jimmy Buffett and choreographed our routines. And as the parents arrived, they each received a handmade floral necklace.

"Wow, girls!" my momma gushed. "The leis are a perfect touch!"

"They sure are," Lauren's momma affirmed. "But where did you get all these flowers?"

"Oh," I said, casually serving up rolls. "The flowers all came from the graveyard."

Momma spit out her pineapple juice. The grown-ups ripped off their leis. The luau was over, without ceremony— a devastating turn of events. And there seemed to be a decided lack of enthusiasm, nay, a repulsed aversion for what I considered a brilliant use of available resources for the luau leis. Some people just don't get your vision when you're a creative.

The next day, I was bored out of my ever-loving mind, playing alone in the backyard. I climbed into the tire swing, stomach down, and flew around looking for bugs. I had just transitioned from bug hunter to Wonder Woman when I heard the side gate squeak open.

"Hey, Lauren," I said, still flying around.

"Hey," she responded. "Wanna play?"

"Yeah," I said, now spinning in circles. "But my mom said we can't go back to the graveyard."

"That's what my mom said, too."

I stopped the swing, and the world kept spinning. Lauren and I sat on the grass.

"What about the playground next to the graveyard? Did your mom say we couldn't go there?"

"Nope," Lauren said, kicking a rock. "She said stay out of the pantry, stay out of the graveyard, and don't make necklaces out of dead people's flowers."

"I don't know why they had such a cow. Dead people don't care about flowers."

• • • • • • •

Let's talk more about Nietzsche. *Thus Spoke Zarathustra* was not a tea-sipping book; I realized that five pages in. It was thick and meaty, and it paired much better with a glass of dry red wine. I'll save you a few bottles (and a good chunk of time) and offer my CliffsNotes summary.

Nietzsche's main character in the novel, Zarathustra, was an übersmart guy who lived in a cave in the mountains. At the beginning of the novel, he was wrapping up a decade spent in solitude. According to Zarathustra, his time as a hermit left his "cup overflowing with wisdom and love." He thus felt compelled to leave his hidey-hole and enlighten the rest of humanity—whom he referred to as, wait for it, *rabble*.

When Zarathustra descended from Mansplainy Mountain, the rabble were conveniently gathered in the town, waiting for a tightrope show to begin. With tension building and a captive audience, Zarathustra saw his big chance. He began speaking and the whole crowd cheered, believing the show had begun.

What happened next can only be described as the buzzkill heard around the world. Zarathustra announced that God was dead and called humanity a laughingstock, then presented the concept of eternal recurrence, which the crowd responded to with laughter. Then, the tightrope walker fell and died. I'm telling you, it was a mess.

Zarathustra returned to his hidey-hole in the mountains, devastated by this turn of events. When I say devastated, I mean it in the most narcissistic way imaginable. His despair came from the idea of spending eternity with the people from town. The very idea distressed him so greatly that he lay on the ground for seven days, unable to eat or drink. When I tell you that I cackled, y'all.

Men call women dramatic.

I didn't care too much for Zarathustra. He was a bit of a mansplainy douchebag. If we met on a blind date at a Mexican restaurant, I would order my own bowl of queso and insist on splitting the check. Zarathustra had problems with both Christians *and* women, making me the most rabble-y of rabble. I'm sure he'd swipe right on me long before dinner. Or is it swipe left? Either way, I can tell you with confidence that Zarathustra was not my people.

Nonetheless, I finished the book (and my merlot), and I will admit it was…intriguing. The culmination of Zarathustra's message is the doctrine of *eternal recurrence*: that we experience the same life, with the same events and experiences, forever and ever, amen. Which sounds wildly depressing. I feel like this concept is the Wish.com version of reincarnation. You find a great deal on an afterlife as a squirrel, and you can't wait for the package to arrive. But it shows up all busted, and smelling like chemicals, and you're stuck being you for eternity.

Anyways, back to the CliffsNotes.

At the end of the book, Zarathustra has finally made peace with eternal recurrence. He even has a group of disciples who share in his beliefs. Understanding that they must experience pain and live alongside the ridiculous rabble, they have accepted that life is indeed worth living—and even more than that, it is worth repeating. They gather in the middle of the night and celebrate with...

THE DRUNKEN SONG.

Oh man! Take heed!
What saith deep midnight's voice indeed?
I slept my sleep—,
From deepest dream I've woke, and plead:—
The world is deep,
And deeper than the day could read.
Deep is its woe—,
Joy—deeper still than grief can be:
Woe saith: Hence! Go!

But joys all want eternity——,
——Want deep, profound eternity!

In the end, my Philosopher Waiter was right. Nietzsche taught me something of joy. It wasn't the nihilistic lesson intended, but I am claiming my truth all the same. The men were all singing that life is full of woe, and woe makes us want to die. But our joy gives life, and it calls out for eternity—deep, profound eternity, as they call it.

I hate to admit it because I don't like the guy, but I agreed with Zarathustra. Life is sprinkled with joyful moments that we wish could stretch into forever.

· · · · · · · ·

When I was pregnant, I cried nonstop; the entire world was upsetting. The intensity of those hormonal meltdowns made everything feel like a serious matter. But I can laugh now, because boy, lemme tell you: My triggers were downright ridiculous.

Shark Tank turned down a teenager, I cried. Taco Bell forgot my mild sauce, I cried. My cat wouldn't come when I called him, I cried. After a few minutes, I would typically recover. But one day, my husband found me sobbing on the couch, curled up in the fetal position. He rushed over to my side to ask what was wrong, and through hiccuping sobs, I unloaded.

"It was an...insurance commercial," I wailed. "It was a

wedding and a baby and an old couple that loved each other. Babe, don't you think life is so beautiful sometimes? Doesn't that make you feel sad?"

Blame it on the hormones; I understand. But there's a reason that sentiment hit me so hard, and it's not how I felt about State Farm. The truth is we know that joy can feel heavy. The most beautiful, meaningful moments in life lodge themselves deep inside of our souls and cause us to wrestle with mortality.

When you first fall in love, you want that to last forever. When you first hold your baby, you want that to last forever. There's a reason wedding photographers command such a pretty penny in our culture. Because we want the feelings of our very best days to stay clear in our hearts, forever.

All joy wants is eternity. Deep, profound eternity.

> **All joy wants is eternity. Deep, profound eternity.**

• • • • • • •

Now, this is where I take the fact that I read Nietzsche for fun and ruin whatever you assumed about my intellect. Because finishing that book, the first thing I thought of was Edward and Bella from *Twilight*. Bella loved Edward so much that all she wanted was to spend eternity beside him. And even though Edward felt the same way, he hesitated to make her a vampire. He believed immortality was a curse, and he didn't want to impart that to Bella. In the end, they have found their happily-ever-after: immortal with a quickly growing child.

Now, this book came out in my early twenties, and this seemed like a fantastic ending. But I'm nearing forty now, and honestly, no thanks. Not that I don't love my husband. We love one another, 'til death do us part, and we fight like hell to preserve that promise. I believe that our marriage will last fifty years, Lord willing and the creek don't rise.

But if Ian and I were suddenly vampires, and our expiration dates disappeared? We'd have to sit down for a serious chat. I'm not so sure we would make it. I told this to Ian, and he laughed out loud. He didn't disagree. I hope Edward and Bella have a really good therapist. Forever is a long damn time.

• • • • • • •

I went back to my family's graveyard this year, but this time I didn't make hula necklaces. Although I stand by the fact that the dead wouldn't care about me using their floral tributes as crafting materials, I have learned to respect social norms. My children, ages five and eight, wanted to know more about their family. So we bought some flowers, picked up my grandfather, and drove over to Maple Hill Cemetery. The weather was cool and the leaves were changing color; it was a beautiful day for a walk. We strolled through the cemetery at my grandfather's pace, stopping to lay flowers on family graves. Neither of my kids had seen gravestones up close, and they were curious about what everything meant. I told them the basics: date of birth, date of death, epitaph, last name. We discussed different wars, the polio pandemic, and various religious symbols. Then Holland walked over to her great-great-grandmother's stone, her little finger pointing out the dash.

"Momma, was Grandma Bea a math teacher? Why does her grave have math?"

"Oh, honey." I giggled. "That's not a minus sign. That symbol is called a dash."

I told her that line, so seemingly small, represented the entirety of life. Whatever happens between birth and death is symbolized by that dash.

I laid some flowers beside her grave and went to go sit by my grandfather. He was resting quietly on a nearby bench, and I could see his eyes were misty. I took his hand, and he squeezed mine in return. There wasn't too much to say.

The children were now running circles around a nearby maple tree. The sun was setting behind the fall leaves, and the trees looked like they were on fire. It was a beautiful moment: the weather, my grandfather, the laughter of my young children. I was having a serious existential moment when my daughter came prancing into view.

"Look, Mommy! I am Te Fiti [from the Disney movie *Moana*]!" she announced with a proud twirl.

My grandfather and I just busted out laughing. Holland sure looked like an island goddess—Grandma Bea's flowers were all in her hair. I didn't say a word, and neither did my grandfather. We both knew that Bea wouldn't care.

· · · · · · ·

Growing up in the '90s, if you were too sick for school, you stayed home alone and watched trash TV. I have no idea where our moms were back then, but I guess they were busy working. One of my favorite shows was *Supermarket Sweep*, which involved a few rounds of boring trivia. But the show got really exciting in the last few minutes, because that's when the sweeps would begin. The teams, all wearing matching sweatshirts, would grab their grocery carts. When the timer went off, they raced throughout the store, attempting to find the most valuable items possible. At checkout, the team with the most valuable cart would win their total in cash.

I would snack on crackers and yell at the families: "Are you stupid? Don't buy the beans! The cereal is more valuable! Go for the chicken!" It was so frustrating to watch teams fail at the sweep. You had to wonder if they did it on purpose. I mean, goodness: The elements to win were so simple. Keep track of your time; memorize the aisles; remember that meat is expensive. But leave it to Team Biscuits to show up to checkout with twenty-five bags full of rice. I wish somebody would

FLOWERS FOR THE DEAD

give me a cart, a few hundred dollars, and a couple of minutes to spend it. I could kill it at this game.

It gets me thinking that we're all competing on some kind of life *Supermarket Sweep*. We've been given a finite budget of time, whether that's thirty-five years, seventy-five years, or a hundred years. And we careen down the aisles of life, spending that budget on what we think is most valuable.

But here's the deal. I've spent far too long and far too much of my time budget loading up on bags of beans instead of the marrow of life. I've trafficked in all kinds of trivial things when real people and experiences were right there in front of me. I've done this because I've thought those things would bring me joy. I've often gone for the bulk when I should have gone for the singular. I've reached for the easy when I should have taken the extra steps for the fortifying.

No, joy doesn't have to be expensive in the ways we typically think. But it's hard to see it there, nestled on the shelf, between the showy and the cheap and the supersized items life throws our way. And it requires the exquisite payment of intention and attention if we're to find it.

I can't help the two of us navigate a journey to joy without acknowledging where we're headed. And where we're headed is...we're all gonna die.

You're welcome. I know that's the premium content you've come here for.

But, for real, that's the deal. We're going to die. And so the quest becomes to find the joy that's here to find. I'm not suggesting we fixate on death, that we become morbid and morose. But we're all playing in the graveyard in the time we have allotted here, dancing above the graves of those who have gone before. And we can use our dash, the space between our births and our deaths, to become relentless joy-seekers, the people who know how to make flower crowns out of grave bouquets. Or we can wallow in the inevitable, trying to distract ourselves from the expiration dates on our lives or giving up long before we should.

There's a song by country artist Tim McGraw that drives this point home for me. I wonder if you've heard it. It came out in the early 2000s, and instantly became a "Live Laugh Love"–type anthem for whiskey-drinking, Wrangler-wearing guys.

The song is called "Live Like You Were Dying." It tells the story of a guy in his forties who finds out that his dad is, well, dying. In the wake of this devastating news, the dying man shares a laundry list of bucket-list items he fulfilled when he got the diagnosis, things like fishing and mountain climbing and riding a bull named Fu Manchu for 2.7 seconds. And he encourages his son to do the same, to live like he was dying.

Tearjerker? For sure.

Some good things to consider? Absolutely.

(Although I think riding a bull is always a bad idea, no matter where you think you are on the mortality sliding scale.)

But, me being me, I gotta question something. The whole idea of living like you were dying? Um, that's right now. It's not living "like" you were dying. We are. Dying, that is. Even when we're healthy. Even when we think we've got lots of years ahead of us. We don't like to think about it, but every morning the alarm clock goes off, we move a day closer to exiting the planet. And of this I have become convinced: It's only when we make peace with our mortality, when we fully accept the inevitability of it, that we can fully engage in joyful living. That means we don't wait for a diagnosis; we go ahead and climb the mountain and love deeper and speak sweeter, right now.

No offense, Mr. McGraw.

I know it sounds counterintuitive, that we find joy by accepting mortality. But think about it. Joy, as we talked about in the last chapter, is a force. And our guy Sir Isaac Newton showed us that forces show up in pairs, the push and the pull, the yin and the yang, the Tom Holland and Zendaya. That means that joy pairs with the knowledge of our brief existences here. The power of the bittersweet. Joy is so compelling *because* it's a choice, a decision that, despite time flying and playgrounds next to graveyards, we see light and connection and relationship and meaning.

If we are indeed on a journey to joy, then the first thing we must understand is where we are going. And friend, whether you are going to Maple Hill Cemetery, you have your ashes sprinkled into the water, or you are beamed up like Scotty (that's what I'm hoping for), whichever way, we have an expiration date. Our dash is what we've got to spend, and we don't know how short it will be. But whether it's twenty dollars or one hundred dollars, don't you want to spend it well?

• • • • • • •

I've been told that where your treasure is, there your heart will be also. I used to believe that people's hearts were where they spent their money. But I've seen cheating husbands buy diamond necklaces for the women whose hearts they were breaking. No, our treasure is time, and where we spend it is where our hearts reside. "I really wish I had worked more overtime," said no dying person, ever. I can agree with Nietzsche on this one thing: Joy wants eternity. And I want to make sure the things I'm pursuing in the name of joy on this finite earth are the things that can go with me into eternity.

Joy eternal.

> I want to make sure the things I'm pursuing in the name of joy on this finite earth are the things that can go with me into eternity.

. . . .

TOUR GUIDE TAKEAWAYS

- Not that I'm encouraging you to read Nietzche. Because I'm not. It was an absolute snoozefest. But what philosophy or opposing opinion has challenged you to rethink your approach to joy?

- Growing up in the South, you collect some weird traditions. Like playing in cemeteries. Did you grow up going to cemeteries and visiting relatives? Or are you deeply uncomfortable at graveyards? What do you think about when you visit a cemetery?

- I get it. We don't like thinking about death, and we sure don't like thinking about our own. But it's a great definer of how we want to live. What do you want your dash to be, that space between your date of birth and the day you leave this earth?

- Have you ever thought about joy being eternal? That it's a connector to the eternity our souls long for? How does it change your perspective on joy? That it's something bigger than the immediate or the mortal?

. . . .

CHAPTER 4

MUDDY MATH

Go down deep enough into anything
and you will find mathematics.
—Dean Schlicter

The day we moved into our first college apartment, Celeste and I were both ecstatic. We were two former cheerleaders from the same little town, with a backlog of shared childhood memories. There weren't octaves high enough to classify our squeals when the very last box was unloaded. We tipped the movers and shut the door, then danced around the kitchen with glee. We felt so grown-up in our very own apartment, with its odd mix of hand-me-down furniture. We wanted to pull our two different styles together under one cohesive look, so we scraped up a hundred dollars between the two of us and went shopping at TJ Maxx.

Strolling through the discounted home decor aisle, Celeste

found a painted canvas. It was a cartoon depiction of a chef from Paris, holding several baguettes. Printed across the bottom of the picture was the word *baguette* in typewriter font. This had somewhat of a Rae Dunn effect, making us squeal with delight.

"Aw, it says 'baguette'!" I said.

"So cute, right?" Celeste replied. "We should do our whole apartment in Paris!"

That was it: We had an agreed-upon aesthetic. We rushed back to the discount aisle with a new sense of purpose. We loaded the cart down with red and black towels, a tiny replica of the Eiffel Tower, and a ginormous picture of a bottle of olive oil.

It said "olive oil" at the bottom.

Because, decor.

Celeste and I did literally everything together. Meal planning, grocery shopping, exercise. When we saw that our local Joe Muggs was hiring a barista, we showed up together to apply for the job. We convinced the manager, a cute guy named Brad, that we could effectively split the position. When Celeste couldn't work, I would cover her schedule. If I needed off, she could pick up my shift. For Celeste and me, things were falling into place beautifully. You'd never seen two happier roommates.

• • • • • • •

The best meal I've ever had the privilege of eating was made in my momma's kitchen. She's a scrappy cook by virtue of necessity, having raised three children on a budget. Not a single ingredient in our fridge went to waste; my mom was an expert food renovator. Yesterday's chicken? Today's chicken tacos. Yesterday's burgers? Today's burger soup. My mother's commitment to a zero-waste home produced hundreds of delicious dinners. But there was one week, one legendary week, when things took a hard left turn.

It all started in Hollywood, I presume, when the producers of the film *Shrek* sat down for a marketing meeting.

"What we need is something a family will use every day that we can make green, like Shrek. Think toilet paper, lunch boxes, underwear—"

"Ketchup!"

"Yes, Stanley! That is genius!"

And that's what they went with. Heinz ketchup, in a sickly shade of green, with a picture of Shrek on the bottle. Now, a quick little aside on thrifty shopping. Most off-brand food is delicious. But when money permits, there are a few key items that are best when purchased on-label. Ketchup is one of the very few items my mom would buy at full price. So, when we saw Shrek ketchup, we begged and pleaded for Momma to put it in the cart.

"I don't know," Momma said. "I'm worried it will taste weird and get wasted."

"No, Momma! We promise! It'll be great! We'll eat it, no matter what!"

That night my mother made her famous meat loaf, with a couple of squirts of sickly green ketchup. We kids were crowding around the kitchen, drawn to the mouthwatering scent. But when Momma pulled the meat loaf out of the oven, there was a collective gasp.

"Ew! What is that?"

"Why is it gurgling?"

"Oh, I don't feel so good."

It was hard to identify what it was, exactly, that Momma was now slicing on the counter. It smelled like meat loaf, but the visual didn't match the olfactory. It was not even close, not even a cousin, of the delicious brown meat loaves of the past. This was something new, and altogether horrifying. It was a gurgling, wet, greenish-brown blob. It looked like the bowel contents of a swamp creature. Maybe Shrek pooped it out.

"What is that?!" my little brother cried out in horror.

Momma responded with a face-melting glare. My siblings and I ran to the table and took our seats in silence. Whatever objections we might have had, Momma wasn't gonna hear them anyway. She tried to warn us about that sickly green ketchup. What was it that we said?

No, Momma! We promise! It'll be great! We'll eat it, no matter what!

And Momma reminded us of that promise, one at a time, as we brought our plates to be served. She served us mashed potatoes, a spoonful of peas, and a huge honking slice of some swamp-green, bubbling beefcake.

• • • • • • •

I left my car running and ran inside my apartment to grab a change of clothes. Celeste was in the kitchen, stirring up a casserole, chatting on the phone. She was dressed in all black, and her apron was on the counter. Joe Muggs barista attire. Not wanting to interrupt her call, I waved hello and went to gather my things. I hoped she hadn't forgotten about the big game. Our sorority's intramural football team had just made it to the finals, and we were scheduled to play Alpha Gam first. Anytime the Pandas were facing the Alpha Gam Squirrels, the chances of drama were high. Which I suppose explains why all the fraternities came to watch. They weren't expecting too much from the football team.

"Hey, MK?" Celeste called from the other room. I could tell something was off. "Can we talk for just a second?"

I pulled on my football jersey and strolled into the kitchen.

"Sure!" I replied. "What's up?—and don't tell me that you are getting ready for work. It's Sorority Super Bowl night!" (Yes, I am an Alpha Omicron Pi.)

"Well," she started. "First of all, you are scheduled to work. You didn't ask off for the game."

I gasped. "No way! What should we do? Doesn't that manager guy from Joe Muggs know our schedules by now?"

"Brad," she responded flatly.

"What?" I asked, confused.

"His name is Brad," Celeste continued. "And it's not his job to know your schedule. It's your job to fill out the requests. Just like it's not my job to work your shift when you decide not to show up. And it's also not my job to do dishes, or the laundry, or the grocery shopping, MK! I don't know what's gotten into you—but you're acting really selfish!"

Thoughts were coming at me at ninety miles an hour. The person she was talking to sounded like a nightmare—but surely that wasn't me. I had my priorities, and backward though they were, Celeste was still high on the list.

"I'm sorry," I started. "I've been a bad roommate. Please don't be mad at me."

Celeste shook her head like she was shaking away a thought. She continued sprinkling cheese.

"I'll cover any shift you ask me to!" I pleaded. "Then will you stop being mad?"

"You were fired last week for not showing up. I took over the rest of your schedule."

"Oh," I said. And there wasn't much else.

"Yeah," said my roomie. "*Oh.*"

• • • • • •

Twenty-four hours after the swamp loaf incident, my family reconvened for dinner. It was spaghetti night and thank God, too. We were in dire need of a makeup meal—a safe encounter with food. What could go wrong with some noodles, marinara, and meat? Spaghetti would be our redemption.

We bowed our heads over empty stomachs, then lined up with our bowls at the stove. Momma strained out some noodles, then pulled the lid off the sauce pot. Delicious smelling steam wafted through the air, causing our stomachs to growl. Momma picked up the ladle and scooped it in deep for a generous helping of sauce.

Splat.

The marinara was a hot, bubbling gray sauce, dotted throughout with pea-green islands of meat. My siblings could not conceal their horror. Even my noodles looked upset. Momma sat down with us at the table and casually offered some Parmesan.

"No thanks," I replied.

"No thanks," said my brother.

"No thanks," said my older sister, Karen Leigh.

Mom raised an eyebrow, twirling her fork. "Y'all always want Parmesan. Is something wrong?"

"Nope," I lied.

"Nope," said my brother.

"Well, we don't want to hurt your feelings, Momma," my sister said, twisting her mouth.

"Oh, please!" Momma laughed. "It won't hurt my feelings. Tell me, what's going on?"

"Our spaghetti looks like roadkill," Karen Leigh said.

Turns out, that hurt Momma's feelings.

• • • • • • •

Three months into our first semester, Celeste asked me to move out. *Asked* is probably too soft of a word; she informed me the locks were changing. It was a roomie divorce for the ages; Judge Judy would have salivated over the details. I got the sofa and the hipster bead curtain; Celeste got the chef with the baguettes.

I signed a rebound lease with another sorority sister, and it had all the trappings of a Las Vegas wedding. We hardly knew each other, but at the end of the day, we were legally bound by the ties of rent, utilities, and cable. I believed this would be my fresh new start. All I needed was to make good grades, start doing dishes, keep my laundry off the floor, pay bills on time, buy my own groceries, and maintain healthy boundaries. I saw zero flaws in this plan for success.

New roommate, new year, new me.

Only, that's not the way things worked out. It was new roommate, new year, same me. The very same struggles with my previous roommate were forwarded to my new address. I was shocked, I tell you, when they showed back up. I guess I thought I'd outrun them.

• • • • • • •

Sometimes, right before I fall asleep, my brain gives me one last scare. It's like:

Hey! Don't go to sleep yet! I found something for you to worry about!

Then it serves up the most offhand memory, but this time it's laced with anxiety.

Remember that comment you made in a meeting this morning? Yikes, that sounded so stupid.

Remember how old Kevin's mom looked in Home Alone? *You're the exact same age now.*

Well, last night, my brain did some serious dredging through the sands of my insecurities, and sure enough, right before I fell asleep, it served up this little treasure:

Remember how you worked in that preschool for two years? You never got Teacher of the Week.

Now, this wasn't exactly new information—but it hadn't bothered me before. I guess I'd never run the numbers to determine how badly I was shunned. But for some reason, right around midnight, that's what my subconscious was doing. And it was all too happy to let me know that something didn't add up.

Fifty-two weeks times two years of employment equals 104 awards. There were only five teachers in the whole school, including you…so did the other teachers win twenty-five times? Remember when they awarded Teacher of the Week to Ms. Sandy in the front office? She never even taught a class. You were either the worst teacher ever, or all those people hated you. Probably both.

Sometimes I think our very worst enemies are the ones inside of our heads. I hadn't thought of that job in years, and here I was, wide awake at one in the morning, chewing my cheek and stressing over the fact that I never got Teacher of the Week. I mean, good grief. Was I really that bad?

I concede, I was terrible at lesson planning and my bulletin boards were hideous, but there was one thing I did better than anyone else in the whole wide preschool: I could bring down the house with my thirty-minute rendition of the "Going on a Bear Hunt" song. That sounds like no big deal, I know, but hear me out: When the weather was bad and the playground closed and the whole school was bursting with energy— all the teachers would pray for a hero, and you know what: That hero was me. Pile those kids into the lunchroom and watch me work my magic. Kids never tire of crawling through gummy-bear forests and swimming across chocolate-pudding moats.

At two in the morning, I made peace with my lack of a Teacher of the Week award. If magical bear hunts were given no merit, the entire system was flawed.

• • • • • • •

When I tell you that I am terrible at math, this is what I mean. Before college started, each student was required to take a standardized test that assessed course-specific competencies. I blew those tests out of the water; that is, except for one. I failed math so hard, so impressively, that the counselor offered a retake. She assumed that my score was so terrible because I'd fallen asleep. I politely informed her that if I'd been napping, I wouldn't have filled in the bubbles. I tried my best and that was my score, and good Lord, how bad could it be?

Pretty freaking bad. I was placed in remedial math, which was essentially high school algebra. I'm sure that would be an easy A grade for most students, but it was a daunting mountain for me. I would later be diagnosed with dyscalculia (math dyslexia), which helped me better understand this struggle. Unfortunately, that diagnosis came too late in life to have any meaningful impact on my studies. In the end, I straight up failed Math Class for Dummies. That F was the final straw on my academic probation, and it meant I was kicked out of school. I remember the pit that formed in my stomach when I sat down to call my parents. I felt so stupid, like such a failure. I thought I would die from embarrassment.

But you know what? I kept right on living.

I'm an author now. The only numbers I deal with are the ones at the bottom of the page. I'm no closer to understanding algebra today than I was the day I was born. God made me a storyteller, not a mathematician. I'm wired to see things differently. So, while remedial math taught me very little about numbers, it did teach me something about life. There was a particular lesson about reducing fractions that has stuck with me all these years. The concept is rudimentary, but its applications are profound (one might even say *remedial*).

This is fractions, so let's start with pie. Also, because everyone loves pie. Let's say that on some alternate planet where I actually know how to cook, I've made two pies, both of them apple. I even bought a gallon of ice cream. I invite you over for dessert and coffee, and we end up talking for hours. At this point you're getting hangry, okay? You are about to chew your arm off. So I ask you how much apple pie you want, and you're like:

"I don't care, MK, just give me some dang pie! That's the whole reason I came over!"

I'm scared of you now, so I run to the kitchen, looking to grab you some pie. But they're cut up all weird and I'm awful at math, so I holler back across the house.

"There's 2/6ths of one pie and 3/8ths of another. Which one do you want me to bring?"

Now, unless you got struck by lightning as a child and have the rare gift of visualizing fractions—this is gonna require some math. Don't worry, friend. I've got you covered. This was one test I didn't flunk.

If you want to eat the biggest piece of pie, well, I guess

you're a greedy friend. Which is fine, I love you anyways. The thing is, you can't really compare these fractions until you understand their parts. The numerator is at the top—it says how many pieces we've got. The denominator is at the bottom, and it's basically like, "Of what, though?"

Well, good sir, I have two slices of apple pie that's cut into six total slices. And I also have three pieces of another apple pie that's cut into eight total slices. Of course, this information does absolutely nothing to help you pick your pie. We are doing an apples-to-oranges comparison, which is dumb with two apple pies. Now, this is where I break out my highest math and *find the common denominator.*

See! Turns out, what we have is 8/24ths of one pie and 9/24s of another. So, take that extra little sliver of pie and stop being grouchy, okay?

If only it were that easy to clearly see the denominator for joy. But our counts are off, and our math is muddy when it comes to the joy economy.

• • • • • • •

I got home from school and saw an ominous box of Hamburger Helper sitting on the counter. I prayed to God that the swamp monster meat wouldn't be making another reappearance. I put my backpack down in my room and went about finding Momma. She was sitting in the den, folding laundry. I carefully minced my words.

"Hey, Momma, I was thinking...You've cooked a lot this week and now you're doing all this laundry, I think you should give yourself a break and order some pizza tonight."

"That's sweet, muffin," she said, discarding a sock that apparently didn't pass the sniff test. "But I'm gonna cook beef stroganoff tonight—and I know it's one of your favorites!"

Momma went back to matching socks, and I knew the conversation was over. I also knew that come 5:00 p.m., her feelings were gonna be hurt. Because if that stroganoff looked even remotely amphibious, I wasn't going to touch it. No matter how many ways she repackaged that meat, it was destined for a garbage disposal.

Albert Einstein once said, "Insanity is doing the same thing over and over again and expecting different results."

That freaking Shrek ketchup. It was the bane of my existence. The source of my family's insanity. It's easy to identify the source of the problem when the source looks like toxic sewer sludge.

But sometimes life takes a hard left turn, and we can't find the source of our problems. What do we do then? When we find ourselves in that third terrible breakup, or financial crisis, or bad job? When we want to have joy, but everything's a mess, and there's no ogre-toned ketchup to blame?

The truth is, math isn't always that simple. There are too many variables at play. And beating mortality only complicates things because it gives us this sense of urgency. We know life is short, but we don't know how short—and we're desperate to make it beautiful. So, we race around life, grasping at straws that we think might solve our problems, acting like we're on a bear hunt for joy. But deeply confused about the nature of what we're hunting.

I've searched for new roommates, thinking joy would be found in the next situation and the next. Another apartment; another roommate; another broken lease. Throughout college, a successful living arrangement felt as likely as winning the Powerball.

I've searched for joy thinking that maybe if I just changed my appearance, I'd feel better and life would be happy. You've done it too? We jump on the crash diet, or get a Groupon for Botox, and wait for the math to work out. Then we're frustrated and hungry and our eyebrows won't wiggle, and it's back to the drawing board, again.

Maybe if I fall in love! That will make me happy! Our whole lives we hear about those elusive "other halves," so maybe a part of us is missing. Then we find our partners, fall in love, and the craziest thing happens. Our relationships strain under the weight of this unspoken expectation. So we look for another variable.

Maybe it's *money*. Financial stress is hard on everyone, right? So we start a side hustle and add a few paychecks, and wait for it to produce some joy. And perhaps we get a vacation or two, which is certainly an added value. But the money gets spent and the relief is fleeting. You can go back and hustle for more, but that is the very definition of insanity.

Doing the same thing, over and over, expecting a different result.

What have you been using as a substitute for joy, the kind of joy that isn't dependent on the next adventure or next acquisition? What's the thing that you've continued to tell yourself: *Well, when this or that happens, then...*? And how many speed bumps have you encountered in the process of chasing that thing?

There are so many obstacles that we will encounter as we journey our way toward joy. Some will be trivial inconveniences—things like flat tires, bad weather, and swampy meat loaf. Some will feel mountainous and impossible to overcome—things like loss, hurt, betrayal.

It can feel like you're trapped inside an eternally recurring bear hunt. Some Nietzschean preschool nightmare. Swish-swash through the marshes of financial hardship; stomp through the forest of complex relationships. Then there's everything else: disease, mental illness, loss of loved ones, faith, the constant droning of the political hellscape. Can't go over it, can't go under it...We seriously must go through it.

How are we supposed to journey to joy when the road is riddled with hazards?

Here's what I've started to figure out: I've spent a lot of time searching for joy in the future. I made *joy* a future-tense term instead of a present-tense one. And now that I've got some life on me, I've also looked back and have spotted joy in the past, and then I've started writing a joy script that sounds like the proverbial "good ole days" kind of stuff I promised I would never say.

But to speak of life and fulfillment, we must keep joy in the present tense. Here. Now. Available.

Sure, I was the uncrowned, unnamed Teacher of the Year for my preschool rendition of "Going on a Bear Hunt." But the secret sauce wasn't all the goofy obstacles I was coming up with for the kids to hilariously navigate. It was that I was fully present with the kids, enjoying every moment, while the other teachers were grousing about the bad weather and watching the clock. I thought it was about my creativity and enthusiasm, but now I see it was that I was *with* my preschool students, vibing with them, making the most of a rainy afternoon.

It's where I blew it with my roommate history, always letting my attention be drawn to the next thing that would make college fun, while missing the friendships right in front of me. And we'll unpack more of the importance of roommates in the next chapter.

I made *joy* a future-tense term instead of a present-tense one.

What I know is this: We can't get a slice of joy if joy isn't the denominator. Whatever fraction of our lives we're spending in the pursuit, if at the end of the day what we're chasing is acceptance or fame or success or safety, then we can slice up that pie a million ways and it will never serve us joy. A pursuit of joy requires going after exactly that, joy, not the things we think approximate it. We can't be surprised when we get served up a slice of something that looks like it was doused in Shrek ketchup if Shrek ketchup is what we pull from the shelf.

Oh, we're on a bear hunt, friend. And here's the good news. Joy is not the bear. Joy is the adventure on the way. Joy is the progress and the friendships experienced in the shared doing, and the giggles and the intensity, the focus and the present. And just like the bear hunt, there are obstacles and challenges along the way, things that will absolutely try to distract us, of that you can be sure.

But if we want to find a big slice of joy on our plate of life, there is a way. And together, we're going to identify what stands between us and it, prepare ourselves for the roadblocks that will hurl themselves across the road, and find out what victory looks like when it comes to living joyfully.

And, I promise, that's all the talk of fractions I'll make. Pinky promise.

. . . .

TOUR GUIDE TAKEAWAYS

Maybe I'm wrong. But I'll bet you've got some kind of repeat story in your life. A repeat story is a pattern you can see in your life, and the revelation is that you're the common denominator. My serial college roommate experience? I was the common denominator. What are some patterns you see in your life that you're starting to discover you in the middle of? It doesn't mean you're the one to blame or the one at fault. Sometimes it has to do with what we're willing to put up with, who we tend to attract, who we tend to be attracted to. But what is your repeat story? And what do you want to do about it?

What's the biggest food disaster you've had to date, when a desired dish didn't live up to its hype? (And this question serves no bigger purpose in our overall search for joy...I just want to know if I'm the only one who had a Shrek ketchup experience.)

We've established I'm no math genius. But it took me a long time to realize that math proficiency, while an impressive parlor trick and certainly good for being a physicist or an accountant, doesn't mean that you'll have a better or more fulfilling life. What is something you were taught you had to have, or you had to do, or you had to be in order to find happiness, but you later realized you didn't need it to find joy?

. . . .

CHAPTER 5

LOST IN TRANSLATION

The noblest pleasure is the joy
of understanding.
—Leonardo da Vinci

cruff McGruff, Chicago, Illinois 60652.

If you sang this jingle in your head, congratulations, you're a child of the '90s. If you are scratching your head because this makes no sense, don't worry; I am here to help. As a bona fide graduate of the D.A.R.E. program (Drug Abuse Resistance Education), I am well-versed on McGruff the Crime Dog. He is iconic, honestly, but I'll give a quick synopsis for those of you who perhaps didn't attend public school. McGruff is an anthropomorphic cartoon bloodhound and the furry face of many crime prevention campaigns throughout the eighties, nineties, and aughts. He would pop up in animated commercials to warn kids about strangers and encourage them to take a bite out of crime. What Smokey the Bear was to forests, McGruff was to municipalities. And sometimes police officers would wear his mascot skin and visit elementary schools.

I don't remember D.A.R.E. taking place on any kind of regular schedule. In fact, I remember my teacher always seeming surprised when the police showed up. You'd have thought it was Santa walking through those doors the way the class responded. It was good ole McGruff and his police officer friend, pushing a bulbous, old-school TV and VCR on a cart. Then, the teacher would push down three or four switches to shut off the fluorescent overhead lights and the room would go quiet in the absence of the familiar background buzzing.

The cartoon was like *Scooby-Doo* but low-budget, grittier, and set on the streets of Chicago. McGruff didn't shy away from heavy topics, either, which made class time even more interesting. McGruff and company taught us all sorts of lessons about kidnapping, drug trafficking, and robbery. It was a little bit heavy for ten-year-olds, sure, but it still beat your whole family dying of dysentery while playing Oregon Trail.

One time McGruff's police officer escort showed us all the different gang signs. To this day, I'm unsure how a police officer in rural Alabama had such in-depth knowledge of said signs. Still, we kids did our part in the fight against gang violence by practicing them on the playground. We knew all about the East Side and the West Side, and I don't mean "of the Mississippi."

D.A.R.E. came to our school on and off for a couple of years, but all good things come to an end. I remember the last time McGruff walked in with his police officer rolling the cart. This time, there was no VCR, just a box full of bright red T-shirts.

"It's D.A.R.E. graduation!" the officer announced. "Congratulations on completing the program!" We signed a pledge that we'd never smoke crack, and in exchange we got the cool T-shirts. (I should mention that many of my classmates went on to wear these shirts ironically in high school, accessorized by bracelets they bought at Hot Topic and reeking of skunky weed.)

With the shirts passed out, the officer debriefed us on everything we had learned.

"If you see a gun, tell the police. If a stranger scares you, tell the police. If anyone in your house is doing drugs. What do you do?"

"Tell the police!"

McGruff clapped at our answer, and he and the officer stood up to leave.

"One more thing," the officer said as he turned back to the class. "My office is next to the cafeteria; you can come by anytime."

• • • • • • •

I've been doing teletherapy for a few years now and have a wonderful relationship with my therapist. Dr. C is a quiet person, but not the jumpy type. If he were like one of those fainting goats, this whole thing wouldn't work. I'm an excitable person, particularly when I'm manic, and I need a therapist who can buffer that excess. Dr. C is an unflappable, still glass of water. I talk to him every Tuesday.

A few weeks ago, at the end of the call, Dr. C leaned in to the camera. "MK," he said. "This week there is something I really want you to work on." Now, in the world of therapy, this statement could go two very different ways. One, Dr. C might give me some emotionally exhausting homework, like writing a letter to myself as a child. Or two, it could be a simple challenge like turning off screens before bedtime. I held my breath, hoping for the latter.

"I want you to be kind to yourself," Dr. C said, and I felt my heart exhale.

"Absolutely, Dr. C! I can do that!"

And for the next six days, I did. Queso for lunch? Being kind to myself! Reflexology massage? Being kind to myself. Wearing pajamas all day, bingeing ice cream and watching serial killer documentaries? *Just doing what the doctor ordered.*

• • • • • • •

Our D.A.R.E. T-shirts were sent home in a bag that was jam-packed with branded swag. I had Just Say No pencils and Just

Say No stickers, and a notebook with a fake bite taken out of it that said "Take a Bite Out of Crime."As I emptied the goody bag's contents into my trash can, a single piece of paper went rogue. It floated across the room and landed faceup on my bedroom floor. It was the very first lesson we'd learned in D.A.R.E., about the dangers of taking drugs. I was about to crumple up the paper and toss it, but something caught my eye. In bold font, at the very top of the page, was the definition of the word *drug*.

Drug: substance which has a physiological effect when ingested or otherwise introduced into the body (examples: marijuana, crack cocaine, alcohol, tobacco, etc.).

I couldn't believe what I was reading. Alcohol...was...a drug? I sat down on my bed with my head in my hands. This was terrible freaking news. I was scheduled to visit my dad for the weekend, and I was very excited to see him. My parents were divorced, and custodial visitation was getting harder and harder to schedule. I loved being with Dad, hanging at his house, cooking out in his backyard. He's a fun-loving, football-watching, Southern kind of dad. And I pretty much worshipped his every move. I would sit in his lap during Auburn games and cheer like crazy for our Tigers. But, during all those games, he always had a cold beer in hand. As if this were totally normal! All along, he'd been drinking drugs, right there with me in his lap. We're talking several cans of ice-cold drugs. A pit formed in my stomach. I promised McGruff I would carry his mantle, and I was a woman of my word.

The next day at recess, I asked Ms. Martin if I could visit the school resource officer. She looked concerned but agreed to let me go. I took her hall pass and went back inside. The rest of the kids could frolic on the playground, but I needed to report a crime.

Yep.

I reported my beer-drinking dad to the D.A.R.E. officer for doing drugs. You're welcome.

• • • • • • •

It was Therapy Tuesday, and I logged in to my appointment, preparing to brag on myself. Dr C asked how I'd been doing, and I couldn't help but smile.

"I took your advice!" I said with pride. "I've been really, really kind to myself."

His eyes lit up. "That's fantastic news! I can't wait to hear about it. Let's do a little exercise, then we will discuss your progress."

"Okey dokey!" I chirped.

"Walk me through the first hour of your day. Internal dialogue, please. What is the narrator in your head like, right when you wake up in the morning?"

Oops.

It was my first inkling that I might have misunderstood the assignment, just a tad. It didn't bode well that we were starting off with internal dialogue. I'd spent the whole week pouring cheese on my feelings, and now I had to scrape it all off.

"Okay," I said, taking a deep breath. This wasn't going to be fun. "First thing in the morning, I look in the mirror. And I think, *Wow, I look really old. And tired. And my teeth are yellow.* Then I sigh with sadness and get in the shower. Usually I look at my body and think of something terrible that I look like. Maybe the Stay Puft Marshmallow Man or one of those whale blubber stress balls. They probably don't make those anymore."

Dr. C leaned back from the screen. "Okay. Please continue."

"Then I get dressed, and usually look in the mirror and tell myself that I'm fat. Then I get my kids ready for school. Usually, I'm in my head thinking how better moms cook eggs instead of Eggos, and don't forget homework assignments. And that better moms wake their kids up early and brush their hair until it shines. So, I rush my kids out the door and drive them up the mountain to school. I drop them off, and tell them I love them, and that's the first hour of my day."

"When you drop them off, any thoughts then?" he asked.

"Yeah," I said, and I could feel tears building. "I just hope I'm not screwing them up."

I could tell that Dr. C was concerned, and honestly, so was I. The self-proclaimed "Week I Was Kind to Myself" didn't live up to its name. I was struggling with some serious hurt, and I couldn't find my way through it. I covered the hurt in cheese dip, but that didn't help. I dulled it with Netflix, but it came right back. And while the massage made my back feel like melted butter, an ache in my spirit remained.

"Dr. C, I feel so lost. I just want to find my joy again."

I found myself crying frustrated tears. I felt trapped in a cycle of misery. How could I possibly fix a problem that I didn't even understand?

"MK," Dr. C replied, "you are a person made of multiple parts. A spirit, a mind, and a body. Your sense of self is kind of like a house—and in it, there are several roommates. When I say you need to be kind to yourself, this is what I mean: Your mental self is mean to your emotional self—you are being your own worst bully."

• • • • • •

I was twenty years old, living at home with my dad, having freshly flunked out of college. My life was out of sorts, and I was searching for something, anything, that would give me purpose. I spent a few months working as a waitress and plugging into a nearby church. I made some friends in a small group, and saved up some money, and then I was invited to this…*thing*. I don't really know how to explain it. It was called One Day, and it was basically Woodstock, minus drugs and iconic music. Now, I was new to the faith, and I didn't yet know that there was such a thing as a Christian celebrity. So while my friends were excitedly rattling off names—Chris

Tomlin, Matt Redman, Beth Moore—I figured that these were their buddies from high school, and maybe I'd get to meet them. To be honest, I am not sure how to describe that weekend. It was certainly one for the books. Thirty thousand adults showed up for One Day, which was actually a three-day gathering. The music was good, the weather was terrible, and I discovered an exciting, new purpose. I felt sure that God was calling me to live out the gospel…in Asia.

"Thailand?" my dad said, holding a globe. He put one finger on Texas. "You realize that's the other side of the planet? Look, the exact opposite side!"

"Of course I know where Thailand is," I lied. "Stop treating me like a child!"

My dad put the globe back in his office, then returned to his comfy chair.

"Here's the thing, MK. I know you're an adult and you'll make your own choices, but remember that you are still *my* child. I don't have to like it that you're going to the other side of the world, but I'll support you."

"You will?"

"Yes, with phone calls and letters. You're paying for this on your own." Two months of paychecks and a garage sale later, I was on a plane to Thailand. This was a prehistoric era before iPhones and laptops, so there wasn't a whole lot to do. Just me, my Bible, a Lonely Planet guide, and a nineteen-hour flight across the globe. I passed the time by studying Thai phrases I would need for everyday life. I learned how to introduce myself, how to count to one hundred, how to ask directions to a bathroom. I learned how to hail a tuk tuk and order fried rice, and how to find internet cafés. Then I moved on to studying cultural nuances that I would need to be cognizant of. For instance, sitting cross-legged in public can be very offensive if your foot is pointed at a stranger. And if you pass by an elder, it's polite to stoop low and quietly say, "Excuse me."

"Kho thot ka," I said over and over. My first stop would be Bangkok, and it would be crowded, and I'd bump into people a lot. It seemed like a good way to establish my presence as a friendly, respectful *farang* (foreigner). A Thai flight attendant walked by, and I was feeling kind of thirsty. So, I took the opportunity to give my very best *excuse me* a spin.

"Kho thot ka," I said and waved politely. But the flight attendant didn't stop. She just smiled sheepishly, gave me a thumbs-up, and hurried to the front of the plane.

It was 8:00 a.m. when we arrived in Bangkok, 8:00 p.m. back in Texas. My host family, the Lekdas, were waiting for me at the airport, with iced coffee and ginormous smiles. They were excited to show me the bustling city, so I chugged a coffee to drown my fatigue. Walking through the airport, I practiced what I'd learned. Lowering my head when I walked by an elder, saying, "Excuse me," when passing close by.

"Kho thot ka," I would say with a smile and a nod. "Kho thot ka," I would say as I stepped out of the way. "Kho thot ka, kho thot ka," again and again.

Now, a foreigner muttering "excuse me" shouldn't have

been a head-turning encounter—but that's the response I continued to get, every time I spoke. Lunch rolled around and the Lekdas took me to a restaurant with beautiful outdoor seating. I played it safe, Diet Coke and fried rice, but I forgot to ask for some spices. So, when the server walked by, in front of the whole dang table, I did my very best "Kho thot ka."

She smiled like she was holding in laughter, and I realized the table was giggling. I decided to ask for my spices in English, and of course she was practically fluent. When the server ran off, I looked at my host family, who were now practically in stitches.

"What did I do?" I asked the table. Was I accidentally giving off some weird signal, like the cross-legged foot thing I'd learned on the plane?

The teenage boy responded, "It's not what you did. It's what you said."

My eyes were as big as saucers.

"I said 'excuse me,' right? That's what I've been saying all day! I thought it was considered polite!"

"Absolutely! But that's not what you were saying. You were asking permission to fart."

• • • • • • •

Do you notice a theme here? Other than my ability to embarrass myself? The thing that derails me, over and over again, is a struggle with communication. I misunderstood the difference between criminal drugs and a casual can of Coors Light. I misunderstood Dr. C's assignment for kindness, not using it as a healing agent for myself. And I traipsed across Thailand asking to fart because I just didn't read the room.

You know what annoys me about this? I absolutely hate it when the central issue in a story or movie has to do with miscommunication. You may watch *Romeo and Juliet* and cry your eyes out. Me? I get screaming mad. What a pair of dum-dums. "Wherefore art thou, Romeo?" How's about "Wherefore art though, follow-up and informational questions?" Why don't y'all gather some clarifying details before taking street drugs from a priest? Come to think of it, Romeo and Juliet might have benefited from a little Chicagoan edge. Scruff McGruff would have asked all the questions and smacked that vial of poison straight from their hands. But I suppose there's a reason this star-crossed story resonates with so many people. So much of our pain is rooted in dysfunctional communication skills.

And here's the kicker for me. I'd like to think that all miscommunication is an outside job. Like, if people could just listen, if they could hear past the noise, they'd understand what I'm trying to say. But as it turns out, the problem originates with how we communicate within. Remember what Dr. C said about roommates? Well, we can't break the lease this time. Somehow, we have to get all of our parts playing nicely under one roof.

Communicating with ourselves is like a ridiculously long game of telephone, where the messages and meanings get lost. All the parts and pieces of me have a hard time hearing and understanding the others. For example, my emotions will get sad. And when they are sad, they demand Oreos. And I hear that and I go straight to the pantry to nosh on a sleeve or two. But then my body pipes in. And it starts saying no, that sugar is not gonna work. It'll send me soaring, and then I'll fall flat, right around the time I need peak energy to go pick up my kids from school. And so my emotions and my body start yelling at each other and I'm somehow stuck in the middle. It's like I'm some metaphysical referee, coaching kindergarten soccer. I want to discern what is really needed, but there's so much chaos and noise. Sometimes I just wanna blow the whistle, eat the Oreos, and call it a day.

For a long time, D.A.R.E. promoted a message of self-esteem as the way to outrun the drug trap. They believed if kids just felt good enough about themselves, they'd avoid a life on the streets. The irony of that well-meaning message is it didn't help that much.

As it turns out, self-esteem isn't necessarily a protective agent, but self-compassion is.[1] Self-esteem is like a little hype man, pumping us up on an endless loop. But self-compassion takes a gentle inventory and sets a foundation for growth.

---

1   Taylor Kreiss, "The Power of Self-Compassion," *Psychology Today*, February 5, 2019, https://www.psychologytoday.com/us/blog/positive-living/201902/the -power-self-compassion.

Self-compassion means we have to be thoughtful about what we say to ourselves about ourselves. It means we're honest about who we are and where we screw up and what we're good at and what we're not good at. But the emphasis is compassion: It means we respond to ourselves with kindness and acceptance, that we show understanding for ourselves. It means we listen for the deeper voice in our hearts, beneath the emotions screaming for Oreos. The voice buried beneath the garbage pile of judgments we've collected along the way.

> Self-compassion means we have to be thoughtful about what we say to ourselves about ourselves.

And you want to know what else I believe self-compassion is? I think it's having clarity on what joy is for *me*. Not what I've been told it is. Not what I think it should be. Not something wildly esoteric or mystically spiritual or hormonally down and dirty. See, I think each of us has a unique code for joy, embedded in who we are. You see the flickers of the code in the longing of your heart. You see the edges of it in a moment of pure laughter. You can almost make out the silhouette of it when you soak in a sense of calm.

It's there. And your joy is ready to speak to you, ready

to tell you what it knows about you. If only the cacophony of culture and expectations and judgment would shut up already.

You and joy aren't star-crossed lovers. You can live your whole lives together. Like soul mates, sitting on the front porch swing, listening to the quiet of the morning. You were made for each other, you and joy. Joy in your relationships with others, joy in your work, joy in your spot in the world, joy in your challenges, joy in your everyday life.

But to find that, to have that, we're going to have to prepare ourselves for the speed bumps we'll hit along the way. They're going to be there, waiting for us. It's part of the human experience. There are nails in the road, landslides across the lane, and dangerous, washed-out bridges. It doesn't mean you're on the wrong track. In fact, it usually means you're on the right track. 'Cause just like my crush Sir Isaac said, there's an equal force and an opposite force at work.

It's time to get your roommates together, 'cause when it comes to this journey to joy, we are stuck in the same dang house. And the last thing you want when you're a thousand miles away is two parts of you fighting over Oreos. Do the work that it takes to have peace in your home (and by home, I mean your whole self). Therapy, psych meds, Jesus, Oreos; it may take a little of each. But when you've got all your parts communicating together, you are ready to set out on the journey. And you and me, we're going to map where the obstacles come up and we're going to come up with some plans. We're going to learn to listen well to and reeducate ourselves about what joy means to each of us.

Joy is bespoke. It's customized. Universal and yet unique. And your joy is trying to talk to you—calling you to you. The question isn't, Can you hear it?

The question is, Are you listening?

> Joy is bespoke. It's customized. Universal and yet unique. And your joy is trying to talk to you—calling you to you.

. . . .

TOUR GUIDE TAKEAWAYS

- One of the things I've worked on in therapy is this habit of talking crap to myself. It's such a habit, it's such a familiar theme song, that I don't often realize the power and the punishment of what I'm saying. What are some things you say to yourself about yourself that you wouldn't say to someone else?

- It's hard to hear joy's call when it's drowned out by my own negative dialogue. What are some things you long for someone to say to you? Be specific. Do you need some love when it comes to the efforts you're making, the body you're living in, the dreams you're nurturing? What about if you said those words to yourself, instead of waiting for someone else to say them? What would your life look like if the voice in your head was kinder? If you said the things you needed to hear?

- Is it hard for you to receive praise? Do you cringe and deflect it when someone sends a compliment your way? Why do you think you do that?

. . . .

CHAPTER 6

A GHOST STORY

Monsters are real, and ghosts are real, too.
They live inside us, and sometimes they win.
—Stephen King, *The Shining*

I love Jesus, but I struggle with community. God knows I have my reasons (literally, He knows). Part of it stems from social anxiety, and part of it is hurt from my past. But a small part might come from my childhood, when I'd have to get up early on the weekends and get dressed for Sunday school.

I hated the dresses, the patent leather shoes, and especially the frilly, fold-down socks. By the time I was dressed, I was over it all, and we hadn't even left the house. For me, the highlight of every Sunday was eating at La Bamba, where my mom let me order my own cheese dip.

One Saturday night, I was dreading church and was wishing we could skip straight to the queso. I asked Momma if

Jesus would mind if maybe we just had church at La Bamba. The people were nicer, we didn't have to dress up, and the food was a serious upgrade.

"I don't like going to church, Momma. But I do want to be a Christian."

Momma smiled. "Going to church doesn't make you a Christian any more than going to La Bamba makes you a taco."

I wasn't quite sure what she meant at the time, but the sentiment was encouraging.

"So, we don't have to get up for Sunday school tomorrow?"

"Lay out your clothes; you're going."

• • • • • • •

Ten years later, I was a newlywed college student looking for a new "church home." Ian suggested we try a few "small groups" (Bible studies that are hosted in homes). I agreed that this sounded a lot less intimidating than going into a big building. So we did a little research, picked a group, and made it a date.

The first thing I noticed when we pulled up to the house was the number of cars out front.

"Good Lord!" I yelped. "There's a million of them. Are you sure we signed up for a small group?"

Ian checked the address.

"Yep, this is the house. Babe, we don't have to go in if you're scared."

My palms were sweating, and my heart was pounding, but I lied and said I was fine. I walked into the house with a Bible in one hand, Ian's hand in the other. The group was friendly, if a little bit stiff. We were ushered toward a large, comfy space. We took a seat on the floor, like the rest of the group, about thirty young adults total.

A lady named Betty opened the group in prayer—and I remember she prayed specifically for our conversation to be vulnerable and honest. The reason I remember is that I heard her words and thought, *Phew, thank goodness. I don't have to pretend!*

The topic was heaven, which I was excited to discuss, and a guy named Sam opened the conversation with a verse from Revelation. He had a picture of God, sitting on a throne, surrounded by shining angels. It was weird because the image looked strikingly similar to an alcoholic family member. Sam read the verse, about angels in heaven surrounding the throne of God. Day and night, they worship Him, singing, "Holy, holy, holy."

"I can't even imagine. They never stop singing!" Sam gushed. "Doesn't that sound amazing?"

Everyone in the room was nodding enthusiastically, and I cut a quick glance at Ian. I wanted to know—I needed to know—if this sounded "amazing" to him. He gave me a look that I surely misread because it seemed to say "Don't say a word." Didn't he hear Ms. Betty praying for the group to be vulnerable and honest?

I raised my hand, and Sam smiled. "Great! A newcomer. Tell us your name! We'd love to hear your thoughts!"

"Hey, I'm Mary Katherine, and uh...spirit of honesty, right? Heaven sounds pretty dang stressful. Singing one word just over and over for thousands and thousands of years? I feel like I'd go crazy, you know. Does anyone worry about that?"

Nobody seemed to share this concern, and I could feel my face growing flushed. My mind started racing and my mouth started moving, and from there, things only got worse.

"Okay, so I know there's no suffering in heaven, but just imagining it gives me anxiety. Y'all remember that show with Lamb Chop in it and the song that never ended? I couldn't listen to it for two minutes. And it's crazy, but that picture of God looks just like my great-uncle. He is not a nice man. He drinks lots of vodka and yells at the kids in his yard. Anyways, I've always imagined God as a lion—you know, like Aslan from Narnia? Human bodies just weird me out, I guess, so I don't think of God like that. Anyways, I hope when I die, I'll go straight to Narnia. I'm a huge fan of talking animals."

My hands got clammy as the silence grew thick. I looked at my husband for a rescue, but he was currently staring at the floor like he wished he could sink inside of it.

"Gosh, it's so fun to have new ideas," Sam said. "Isn't it fun, everyone?"

The room was torn between head nods and golf claps, and I wanted to turn into sand.

• • • • • • •

It was a Thursday night the first time it happened.

My family and I were all eating dinner in the den and watching whatever Disney movie was free on Netflix at the time. My son Ben was two years old at the time. He stood up from his perch on our indoor picnic blanket and crossed the room to cuddle up in my lap.

"Hey, baby," I whispered, running my hands through his spectacular curls. The end of the day was my favorite time with him at that age. He was just tired enough to be extra snuggly, but not so tired that he was a holy terror.

"Mommy," Ben whispered. "I think our little girl is sad."

I placed my hand over the place in my stomach where his little sister was growing inside me. We were just now beginning to explain the concept that the bump in Mommy's tummy was an actual human whom he would soon be able to hold and even play with. I figured the big brother was trying to connect with his soon-to-be sibling, and my heart instantly melted.

"Awww, baby! Little Sister isn't sad. She's happy! She's super happy because she has such an amazing big brother like you!"

My son shook his head gently, casually shoving another Pringle into his mouth.

"No, Momma," he said, munching on his potato chip. "Not Little Sister."

Um, okay. I'm gonna have to get some clarification here.

"Honey, then which little girl is sad?"

Without missing a beat, he responded: "The little girl who sleeps in our house."

'Scuse me?

Pause with me for a second. My child was two, folks. Pretty sure he didn't get this idea from Disney Junior. And despite his impressive Play-Doh snake-making skills, I was pretty sure he wasn't creative enough to make something like this up.

And it quickly got worse.

Ben raised his finger, pointed behind the chair in which my husband sat, and added: "Right there, with the red eyes."

It was at that moment I experienced what can only be described as all the nopes that ever noped. My blood ran cold, and I suddenly felt an urge to pack our things, light a ginormous match, and burn the house down as we peeled out of the driveway. I half expected to see the little old Southern lady from *Poltergeist* waving goodbye in my rearview. *This house is clean...*

We could start all over in a different city. Any city. I was ready to go. Who cares if we just bought our dream house? There is no gas stove, no pool so awesome that it's worth living with a red-eyed baby demon. None of my babies, inside or outside of my belly, would be getting Carol-Anned on my watch.

Really, though, what in the cornbread hell are you supposed to do when your kid drops a bomb like that?

I'll tell you what I did: I ended that picnic without cere-mony and carried my son's creepy little butt up to bed. Then I returned downstairs, very much expecting all my cabinets and drawers to be open. Upon establishing that the coast was clear, I sat down to google "how to get rid of ghosts" (which, I must say, yielded a mixed bag of helpful, hilarious, and terrifying advice from the quirky people of the internet). Here is what I discovered:

First, you have to rule out "nonparanormal" possibilities. Okay, check. We don't live near a dumpster, so rats and rac-coons are not currently scratching at our roof every night, and even if they were, I don't think my son would confuse said scratching for an ominous spectral child. So once again, thanks for nothing, Wikipedia. We still had a ghost problem.

Second, the people of the web recommended that we make "friendly contact" with the spirit. Now, I consider myself a pretty open person, but I'm going to admit I carry a small prejudice toward red-eyed crying dead people. If Casper floats through my wall and makes friends with my child, then sure. I'll be more than happy to have a friendly word with his adorable, bald little ghost face. But I've seen enough (about twelve minutes) of a paranormal-activity movie to know how that progression goes. If some shadowy form throws me across a room, y'all can call the coroner right then. I'll be dead. So friendly conversation was off the table, which left us with option #3: exorcism.

And yeah, no thanks. I've already seen that movie, had the

nightmares, and got the pea-soup-covered T-shirt. Find me an exorcism story with a happy ending. I'll wait. Forever. Because there ain't one.

I continued clicking for about an hour: scrolling, reading, and shaking my head at the devastating lack of explanations available for "red-eyed ghost child in the corner of my family room." I even stumbled upon an essential oils thread (because of course), and imagine my disappointment when even the oiliest of mommas couldn't offer me a cure for the undead. (I can't wait for the next time my local oils dealer tells me that crap "cures everything.") Defeated by my lack of options and pretty frantic that I was about to close my eyes and sleep in a house that was possibly cohabitated by a crying ghost child, I did the most desperate thing a parent can do:

I consulted Facebook.

Now, pause for a moment to consider just how desperate someone must be to put on blast, "Hey, y'all. My kid just saw a demon-faced girl in the corner of our den, any recommendations?"

But I was exactly that desperate, so I hit Post.

And I waited.

And to my shock (and slight relief?), I didn't have to wait very long 'til the responses came flooding in.

I was bombarded with stories of postfuneral sightings, historic house hauntings, you name it. One momma commented that her three-year-old twins once sat down for a pretend tea party with a woman named Magdalina. No big deal, right? Well, Magdalina happened to be the name of their late great-grandmother who died two days before their birth. Their mom never really talked about her, but one day she was just sitting in the kitchen cooking grits and overheard the girls giggling.

"Oh, come sit down, Magdalina! We have your favorite tea, Magdalina!"

And two-point creepy bonus? They poured her a cup of her actual favorite tea: vanilla rose.

The anecdotal evidence was continuing to pile up around me, and I was actually relieved to know I wasn't flying solo with this disturbing issue. Ian gave me multiple side-eyes, mumbling that of course I would find comfort in anecdotal confirmation of our son seeing a ghost. My particular brand of crazy does love company. As more and more parents reached out, I was inspired to do a little research on my one-hundred-year-old home.

And wouldn't you know, there was once a little girl that lived here in the 1900s.

She even had red eyes.

Okay, I'm just kidding. That didn't happen. But what did happen was that my son continued to have "sightings" of this girl, whom he affectionately dubbed "Night Night Angel" because all this terror sundae needed was a creepy cherry on top. And one night, I was finally brave enough to ask him if I could meet his little, um, friend.

He smiled like the little angel he is and took his momma's

hand, then walked me over to the wall where he had apparently located the nexus of his ghost sightings.

"Night Night Angel!" Ben chortled, pointing a chubby finger behind the couch. And that's when I saw the two little lights, which, thank heavens, weren't attached to a face. They were simply a projection from our entertainment system onto the corner of the wall.

• • • • • • •

I'm convinced that God has a weird sense of humor. Have you seen the duck-billed platypus? Not only does it look like some duck-beaver hybrid, but it's a walking contradiction. For one thing, it's a mammal but it also lays eggs. It's furry but it has duck feet. And then, it's oddly adorable, but at the same time, has highly dangerous venom. Did you know that the male platypus can deliver what scientists call a mega-sting? It sounds terrible because it is. The mega-sting delivers excruciating pain comparable to being attacked by hundreds of hornets. Now I have to be honest with you: I didn't have "potential to kill or incapacitate" on my platypus bingo card. I've got a long list of "how" and "why" type questions I'm going to ask God when I meet Him. And while the platypus is interesting, he's not very high on the priority list. I'd say roughly page 8.

A bigger question I'd like to ask God is why He created me as an extrovert with debilitating social anxiety. I love people. I need people in my life. But, I'm kinda allergic to them, too.

This typically results in me going into social gatherings, making things weird for everyone, including myself, and not knowing how to recover. I call this condition verbal diarrhea and it feels about as gross as it sounds. For instance, this condition would be things like announcing to a small group that heaven sounds boring, and I'd rather be around talking beavers.

Ahem. For example.

My husband has social anxiety, too, but his plays out much differently. Ian doesn't get loud or obnoxious or weird like me. He gets quiet and small, retracting inward like a hermit crab in a shell. It would seem like we are polar opposites, but the truth is we wrestle with similar enemies. We both struggle with a soul-deep insecurity. And while we express it in different ways, Ian retracting and me spewing, it all comes from that same place.

Do these people like me? Can I make them like me more? Am I blowing it? Am I the weirdo in the group? Why does this feel exactly like that group of girls at the lunch table in seventh grade? Maybe I should say more? Something funnier? Something bigger, louder? Should I just shut up? What if none of them like me ever and no one ever likes me again and I die alone sprawled akimbo on an olive-green shag carpet?

You know, thoughts like that. As one does.

All it takes for me to go into this kind of spiral, and all it takes for Ian to head into his own brand of spiral, is one last, tiny snowflake landing on Mount Insecurity and the avalanche begins.

It makes you never want to risk being around the species *Homo sapiens* ever again.

• • • • • • •

Look, I'm here to own some mistakes and tell you the stories about them so that maybe, perhaps, you don't have to go through the same stuff or go through it for as long. Because the thing is, we've got to have community to come into a fuller experience of joy. We are hard-wired for human interaction. But if we're not mindful, we can sabotage the heck out of things. Like that kid that pokes a single domino, then cries when the rest of them fall. There are things in our lives with cascading effects that can block our path to joy.

> There are things in our lives with cascading effects that can block our path to joy.

It's all connected, just like Kevin Bacon is somehow connected to every other Hollywood celebrity.

The first domino poker in my life is insecurity. I talk myself into believing that community is scarce, which in turn makes me feel insecure. I end up tied in all kinds of knots, convincing myself that there aren't enough friendships to go around, and if I don't outjoke, outtalk, and outshare, then

I'll miss the community bus. And once I do all that oversharing mess, then I talk myself into reanalyzing every moment and beat, convinced I've blown it with this latest group of people. This mindset of scarcity creates insecurity that, in turn, makes community scarce. There's this dot of fear that I roll over in my head, over and over again. I study it and fixate on it and convince myself that I'll get hurt, and then I fill in the narrative from there. Fear begets loneliness begets fear begets loneliness; it's a circular, self-fulfilling prophecy.

Like my old pal Night Night Angel. That whole terrifying story started out with two very real red dots on a wall. Call them painful past experiences or valid anxiety—but those dots are our insecurities. And what we do next is take our little finger and draw the outline of ghosts. We fill in the narrative that we are sure will inevitably unfold, then we allow that story to haunt us.

Let me tell you, I can write motives and inner dialogue where it flat doesn't exist. Remember that church small group I was convinced hated me after my heaven/beaver pontifications? People in that group contacted us afterward. Not that I answered my phone. Still, they left messages saying how fun the conversation was, and they enjoyed getting to know us, and they really hoped we'd come back.

But because I was operating out of insecurity, where they saw humor and a potential friend, I remembered head nods and golf claps. In the end, I exchanged the direct messages they sent my way for the ones I had written. The cycle of scarcity continues.

Friend, if you deeply crave joy in your life, if you really want to experience it consistently, as a lifestyle, it's going to take making community not just a priority, but a risk you're willing to take.

Will you get hurt along the way? Definitely. Will you have times you overtalk, overshare, undershare, panic, or hide? Chances are also pretty good.

But…finding your people is awkward.

Let's face it, walking into a room where you don't really know anybody and beginning the dance of conversation is… weird. *"Hi! What do you do, what do you like, what do you not like, do you always dress like this, how could you possibly like that movie, you run how many miles a day, wow that's impressive, sometimes I run to the bathroom."*

I imagine these conversations have been awkward since the beginning. I can't imagine being Adam and Eve.

"Hey, cool body; mine is different, but let's be friends. Want to name that animal over there? Oh, I was thinking Danger Noodle, but snake sounds fine. Have you heard of this cool new tree in town? I hear it has the best apples."

> If you deeply crave joy in your life, if you really want to experience it consistently, as a lifestyle, it's going to take making community not just a priority, but a risk you're willing to take.

Peopling is hard, because you're reaching into the unknown, trying to make a connection. It's vulnerable and scary; it's a little unclear and uncomfortable.

Until it isn't. Until you find your people.

Hold on for that moment. Because you will find them. We're built for it. It's literally in our DNA. You may need less community than some or you may need more. You may like folks who are a little more contemplative or you may love to hang with big personalities who bring down the house.

Whatever your taste, you can't tell me that in the whole wide world of more than 7.5 billion people, there's no place and no people for you. There is. But too often we exchange our deep need for community and its symbiotic relationship to joy for staying safe or unseen or cushioned from possible rejection. We tell ourselves ghost stories about what happened last time we tried to be part of that mom group or what might happen if we introduce ourselves to that family who moved in next door.

But as long as you operate from insecurity, the joy in your life will be scarce. You might have some moments here or there, but it won't fill your life to the brim. And who wants a life that is "just enough" joy. You want crazy joy, the kind that fills up every room in your heart and explodes through the windows of your soul.

So I'm asking you, begging you: Take the risk. Let go of the ghost stories you've been telling yourself and get out of the dang house. Friendship is out there, ready to be experienced—if you can let go of your insecurity. Step out of the scarcity mindset and look for your people.

What you'll find is joy in abundance.

> You want crazy joy, the kind that fills up every room in your heart and explodes through the windows of your soul.

TOUR GUIDE TAKEAWAYS

- So, obviously, I can make a small-group discussion a little wild. But I still stand by my concerns that hanging around heaven in a never-ending choir rehearsal is not exactly my idea of paradise. What is something you've said, out loud, that you still stand by...but it left a bit of an echo in the room?

- What is a ghost story you've been telling yourself over the years? Some haunting insult that you assume others are thinking?

CHAPTER 7

DRAGONS
AND BRIDGES

The hardest thing in life to learn is which
bridge to cross and which to burn.
—David Russell

I decided to take the kids out for ice cream before a playdate
at their friends' house, and like every other time I do something spontaneous and awesome for them, they rewarded me
by fighting one another from their car seats.

"Holland farted!"

"No, I didn't!"

"Ben touched me with his foot!"

"I was just stretching my leg!"

You know, the usual. So, I did my best to distract my offspring with this superclever game of "Oh, look at this random
thing I see in the parking lot."

I pointed out a broken shopping buggy, a man dancing with an oil change sign, and a blackbird eating a french fry. The parking lot was PACKED, y'all. Ten minutes later, I was finally inching up to the exit when my more imaginative child yelled,

"I SPY A DRAGON, MOMMY! LOOK!"

So, I pumped the brakes because we were in FLORIDA. We were living in the Orange State at the time. It's practically Australia but with more retired people and minus the lovely accents. A parking lot alligator wouldn't be unheard of.

"Where is it, baby?" I asked, looking around the car for any signs of dragon-type creatures.

"Right—THERE! MOMMY! NO! A CAR JUST SQUASHED IT!"

Oh, OF COURSE.

OF. COURSE.

I put my car in park, which immediately pissed off the six people behind me, and I rolled down my window. I peeked back and, sure enough, a partially whole, two-foot-long lizard thing was lying in the middle of the parking lot exit.

First of all, I hate reptiles. HATE. I just got a full-body chill even typing the word *reptile*. It's either the scaly skin, the flicking tongues, the way they can dart across a room like Chucky, or all of the above.

But the only thing I hate as much as a green, scaly mystery creature is the idea that it might be suffering. I have a real problem with trying to save animals that already have one paw or claw through the pearly gates. Ask me about the time our cat ate half a backyard bunny, and I tried to bring the other half to our vet. So, against my better judgment and my momma's voice loudly scolding in my head, I hopped out of the car and into the line of traffic.

JUST in time to stop the ole boy with the mud-tire truck from further mincing the poor creature.

"STAHP! STAHP! Can't you see he's suffering?" I yelled, not in a dramatic way that would concern strangers or make me wind up on YouTube. Ahem. Not at all. Except…yeah.

The line of cars stuck behind my vehicle was only getting longer while I was assessing the situation, and everyone looked super agitated. My son rolled down his window to yell at me for being in traffic because he didn't want me to get hurt—even though HE was the reason I was in this mess to begin with. No one else seemed concerned about the well-being of this ugly-as-sin creature, which says something about either me or the world.

My soul: *We have to save this creature.*

My brain: *There is a box in the backseat.*

My mouth: "*very long string of expletives*"

So, I directed traffic around this dang thing, and I was frankly not even sure what it was. It had red spikes and was longer than my forearm, and even though I've heard lizards can regrow tails, this one was looking pretty rough with, like, tail guts or *something* coming out. The regeneration of guts is not something I'm widely familiar with.

I removed one sandal and scooped the lizard into the box I'd retrieved from the back of my mom wagon, arms fully extended away from my body. Empathy be damned, keeping every possible inch between this parking lot dragon and the rest of my person was of the utmost importance.

I was hyperventilating. This was not okay.

Mud Tire Guy would surely help me. He looked like the manly-man-rescue-the-lady type. So I tried my best to look helpless and squeak out:

"Sir, can you take it to a hospital?"

He pulled his truck past me and tipped his hat.

"Hail nawl, little lady. That thang is all on you."

The line of cars followed suit, swerving around this lizard triage scene, and pretty soon I was standing alone, next to my car, with a half-dead mini dragon in a shoebox that was IN MY HANDS.

no no no this is not okay somebody else has to do this I am not doing this

But I did.

I got in my car and set the lizard box on my center console, and my children were now screaming in a combination of horror and excitement.

"MOMMY, IS IT GONNA GET OUT? DON'T LET IT DIE!"

"Don't let BooBooZilla die!"

Awesome. Great. They named the parking lot dragon in the shoebox in my car. Once your kids name something, be it animal, vegetable, or mineral, you cannot let it die. If it wasn't already, this lizard was officially my burden to bear.

So I called my friend and was all casual-like. "Hey, I know we have a playdate and you have your twins all by yourself, but how do you feel about me dumping two hangry kids on you for an hour so I can drive this partially dead dragon thing to the exotic animal hospital?"

And without so much as a "Huh, what?" she agreed. My friends are either loyal or certifiably nuts. Or they just know me well enough that my moonlighting as a reptile EMT does not surprise them in the least.

As I dropped the kids off, Holland wished BooBooZilla well and was making plans to rehabilitate him herself at our house. My friend gave me the eyebrow raise that friends only give you when they know they're not allowed to bust out laughing in your face. I tried to ignore the intense crawling sensation overtaking my skin as I pulled out of the driveway, glancing down at the box to make sure the tail guts weren't leaking.

"Siri, call animal hospital!"

I was using the voice command with my phone on the dashboard because I didn't want to be a distracted driver.

But it's hard to NOT be distracted by a two-foot-long wild animal in your cup-holder vicinity. And so I almost missed the red light, which caused me to slam on the brakes, sending my phone flying to the floorboard.

Instinctively, I mom-armed the damn box, which sent my

body into one hundred percent panic-attack mode because my brain immediately played out ten thousand scenarios involving a flying lizard, my windshield, tail guts, and my arm.

I wasn't okay. I checked on my tiny little dragon, and he didn't seem super okay, either.

"Oh no you don't, BooBooZilla! STAY WITH US! STAY WITH USSSS!" I yelled. He opened one little yellow eye and blinked.

He was fading. Fast. But after all I went through, he was NOT allowed the luxury of death.

NO SIR, NOT TODAY.

"STAY WITH US, BOOBOOZILLA!"

I peeled into the vet parking lot, grabbed the box, and ran to the door with my arms outstretched, for fear he might suddenly feel better and fly out at me like a spider monkey.

"I HAVE AN ANIMAL EMERGENCY!" I announced as I rushed toward the receptionist. Placing the box on the counter, I stepped back and crunched over to breathe.

"Can you save him?"

The receptionist didn't even look at me when she asked: "Is this…BooBooZilla?"

"Yes—uh, how did you—?"

"Well, you called."

I called?

OH MY GOD, I CALLED.

My phone had dialed the vet clinic and had kept the connection through the red-light flying situation. So, I had the not-at-all shameful experience of sitting in a waiting room for twenty minutes, filling out paperwork for an animal rescue while sharing oxygen with a stranger who heard me frantically yelling, "STAY WITH US, BOOBOOZILLA!" in my car.

When the lizard was finally safe in the vet's care, and my paperwork was complete, the receptionist lady asked me if I wanted the box back.

No. No, I did not.

I thanked them for their help and told them I would call to check in on BooBooZilla soon.

The next day, my kids were clamoring for an update, so I rang the vet to ask how the dragon and the remainder of his tail was doing.

"We're sorry, but the iguana had to be euthanized."

Wait, what? I knew he didn't look well, but surely he wasn't so bad that there were no options left. Even if he had to lose more than just the tail, couldn't they give him one of those little wheelchairs that dogs with no back legs use to get around? Or was there something I should have done at the scene of the accident, some kind of lizard trauma triage?

"Wild animals aren't really made for wheelchairs, ma'am. We wanted to talk to you about this. We saw that prior to this iguana situation, you brought in a bunny you found."

"Oh my goodness! Harry Buns Piglet? Do you mind if I ask how he's doing? It's been a while since we've gotten an update."

I then received a gentle but firm talking-to about my wild animal rescue habits and the limitations of what a vet for domesticated pets can actually do when you come flying in the door with creatures you're trying to save from becoming roadkill.

Turns out that despite my well-intentioned efforts, I wasn't rescuing a gosh darn thing.

• • • • • • •

A few years back, footage of a Minneapolis bridge collapse was aired on national television and cars—with actual people in them—dropped into the river like Matchbox toys.

Driving over a bridge nowadays, I feel like a feral cat trapped in a metal box. All I can see are tiny cars: falling, falling, falling.

A bridge is a thing of beauty. A triumph of modern engineering. But I don't have to trust one—and I never will.

And that is my thing with bridges.

Then, not long ago, a bridge I was driving on collapsed.

No, not literally. It was a relationship that I valued, a bridge that linked me to a sense of community and trust and camaraderie. It failed, crumbled, and collapsed with a quickness. And as my little car of a heart was nose-diving for the river, I couldn't help but wonder:

What just happened?

I loved this person. I really did. But the friendship was in rubble and love wasn't enough to fix it.

I've heard it said (and sung) that "love can build a bridge." And perhaps that is true. But why, then, do so many marriages, friendships, and partnerships fall apart?

Because without a reliable foundation and infrastructure, relationships are destined for failure. Without accommodations made for the wind that the bridge will often encounter, without accurate estimates of what loads the bridge can handle, heck, even not taking into consideration the wear of time and environment a bridge will be subjected to, it can all come crashing down, even with love still being part of the equation.

Love can most certainly build a bridge. But, as it turns out, love is a crappy engineer.

If you've ever seen or experienced a whirlwind romance, you know what I'm talking about. Built so quickly. So excitedly. But when it experiences actual weight, that's when the implosion occurs. By then it's too late. And it's not just whirlwind romances that are at risk. Even relationships that have a long shelf life can go bad over time.

And it reminds me of the importance of being a bridge inspector.

There are more than six hundred thousand bridges in the US, and check this out: Almost half of them are over fifty years old. So the clock has been ticking on many of the bridges you and I cross every day. Not only that, but it's estimated that over 7 percent of the bridges in the US are considered unsafe, not reliable for us to use to cross troubled waters.[1]

Talk about nightmare fuel. People drive over these bridges almost 180 million times every year, with no idea what is crumbling beneath their wheels.

Look, it's nearly impossible to stay on the road to joy if you're using unsafe bridges to try to get there. The quality of your joy is directly related to the quality of the relationships in your life. And if the road to your connections is paved with toxic asphalt, subject to the elements and harsh conditions of life, you may find yourself plunging into perilous crevices of loneliness, abuse, gaslighting, and all the rest of the unholy cornucopia that is the stuff of fractured friendships.

We are human. Wrecks happen. Sometimes those wrecks happen before we start crossing a bridge, and if we are lucky, a wreck can reveal the weakness in a relationship before a total collapse occurs.

And that's when we have two choices:

1. Grab a hammer, say a prayer, and get to work repairing the weaker parts.
2. Assess the damage. Say, "This has gotten bad enough," and find another road.

---

1   ASCE (American Society of Civil Engineers), "Overview of Bridges," 2021 Report Card for America's Infrastructure, https://infrastructurereportcard .org/cat-item/bridges.

Either way, it's painful when things break. Both parties are left there, mending wounds and wondering how they never saw it coming.

So what do you do—when it's you standing there, confused in the rubble?

Give it time. And when the dust finally settles…go find the point of failure. Study it. Take responsibility for your part in it. Identify that common denominator of your part in the equation. Forgive the other person's part in it.

And the next time you find yourself building something great, thinking it's going to be the route to span you over to your happiness, be careful not to repeat the same mistakes.

• • • • • • •

Apparently, wild animals aren't super adaptive. Especially partially squashed road dragons. They're wired to be wild. As my slightly exasperated friends at the vet clinic reminded me, once you introduce them to the domesticated world, they can't be unintroduced. Their brains are wired to keep their distance from people and fear humans because that is how they stay safe. Fear of humans is an important instinct that helps animals survive in the wild. But after they get yanked out of their environment—say, scooped into a shoebox and thrown in the center console of an SUV that's 30 percent Goldfish crumbs—the way they interact with the world is fundamentally altered and there are only two options left. Either they are shipped off to a wildlife center where they will remain captive forever, or, if that isn't a feasible option, they will be euthanized (rest in peace, BooBooZilla).

Now, I haven't been half-eaten by a domesticated panther descendant or run over by a mud-tire truck, but I've had more typical human versions of trauma, and have the therapy bill to prove it. One of the things I've learned in therapy is that our brains do something similar with trauma. When our environment is made up of people who are supposed to be safe, the ones who are supposed to love us, but those people turn out not to be safe, it rewires our brains to accept or even seek out unsafe people. It normalizes unsafe behavior toward us.

But here is the difference: We are not fundamentally altered. *We can heal.* And if we want to have joy in relationships, we must take steps toward that healing. Through therapy, medication, and showing up for ourselves, we can repair the damage trauma has done and retrain our brains to expect more from the world around us. Carlos Santana once said, "If you carry joy in your heart, you can heal any moment."

Look at the relationships in your life. Do they fill you with joy, or do they cause you pain?

The people you've chosen to love or even the family you were born into—is it possible that they've been trying to domesticate you in ways that have left you hurt? If you hold the way your people treat you up to the light, do support, kindness, and love shine through? Or are there watermarks of harshness, dysfunction, rejection, agenda, or trauma embedded in the fibers?

While I passionately believe that deep, honest relationships are a critical part of the joy recipe, it can't be just *any* relationships. Forged, assumed, assigned, or otherwise. Love should build up and not intentionally hurt.

There are environments that are toxic for you and me. There are wild places in our hearts that are meant to be treasured and valued, not domesticated. And if there are people in your world who are trying to cage you in, change what makes you wild, or squeeze the joy out of you, well, it's time to move away from those people. Love them from afar, wish them the best, but don't subject yourself to more hurt or being made to feel smaller than you are.

I'm telling you, the kind of joy you'll experience when you take the risk and retire some of the gatekeepers around you, well, there's nothing like it. The people who get your weird humor and delight in your debates and know how to let you be quiet and how to let you be loud, all while you do the same for them, it's a revelation.

I get it. You're scared to get up and try again. You're tired. Maybe your heart's still a little banged-up. But

> The kind of joy you'll experience when you take the risk and retire some of the gatekeepers around you, well, there's nothing like it.

your people are out there, the ones who will watch your kids while you run BooBooZilla to the vet. The ones who will do the hard work with you of repairing those broken bridges. Who will cheer you on in your journey to joy and will remind you that all the things that make you unique are exactly, ironically, why you fit together.

Don't stop crossing bridges, friend. They carry you deeper into the land of joy. But inspect those bridges. Engage in the required maintenance. And if you find that the foundation isn't there, bless it and let it go.

While you may not have been in any way responsible for your past hurts, you are responsible for your healing. Be proactive and seek out the help you need to rewire your heart and mind. So you can freshly define what is safe and life-giving and beneficial for you.

The best bridges are built when there is mutual trust, solid foundations on both sides. If a bridge is broken and hurting, you need to ask yourself: *Is this something I should work to fix, or should I let this lizard lie?*

And this is where I remind you, one more time: Love shouldn't hurt. Peace is found in the kind of community that's both safe and mutually supportive.

If you want to go further in your journey to joy, then you can't accept anything less.

- -

TOUR GUIDE TAKEAWAYS

- How do you know when you're trying to cross bridges to relationships that are unstable, that are swaying and twisting beneath your feet?

- What relationships have you tried to "save" that should have been lovingly extinguished? Do you carry a belief that it's your responsibility to make any and every relationship work? Or do you blow anyone out of the water who doesn't do things your way? What does balance look like to you?

- I confess, I've had times when I've expected a friend to be a stable bridge beneath my feet while I was anything but a safe harbor to them. Somehow, we've got to honestly bring our crazy to relationships while not making the relationship crazy. Joy is found in being fully known...and in knowing how to make room for the other person. What do you think are some good practices that will help you bring your whole self to a friendship without making that friendship one-sided?

- -

CHAPTER 8

THIEF OF JOY

You are entitled to feel all the bitterness
and hatred you were taught. You are entitled
to carry with you the pain and sorrow,
the longing and disappointment.
They will happily accompany you through
life. Claim them if you will, but remember
they are greedy, and their demands
are many. You must be ready to pay
the price they require.

—Tracie Peterson and Kimberley Woodhouse,
All Things Hidden

think by now it is well established that I'm a believer in the
magic of Christmas. I have some deeply instinctual connection to winter, like one of those migratory birds. Except I
don't leave town when the air gets chilly—I bust out my col-
lections of tacky sweaters, hang up a million lights, and ready

myself for the holiday season. The most wonderful time of the year.

Everything about Christmas is magical to me: the trees, the stockings, the story of Jesus, the neighbor's inflatable Snoopy. It's hard to say what I love the most when the world is a winter wonderland—but there is one tradition that in recent years has come to stand out as a favorite.

In my study, there is a woodburning fireplace that stays lit all winter long. Frequently, at the end of the day, I will tuck my children into bed and crash on the sofa across from that fireplace, sipping something hot. In the height of the pandemic, I did this nightly. It was such a balm to the soul—not just the relaxing, flickering flames, but the pictures lined up on the mantel.

Is there anything as joyful as a family Christmas card? The amazing photographic evidence of rings and vows newly exchanged, the new babies who landed earthside in the last year, and the babies of years past who suddenly aren't babies anymore. It's so incredible to see your people and their people growing up through the years, celebrating the holidays, all color coordinated and spit shined. These pictures serve as evidence to me that my people are still out there, even when we aren't together. Just seeing their joy (and their adorable pajamas) is enough to fill me with gratitude.

Most of the time.

One night, after a particularly bad day at work, I sat down for this nightly ritual. School was shut down, and I was behind on my manuscript, and I'd been struggling with a bout of depression. I figured some fire gazing and staring at cards would serve as a balm to my spirit.

But this time when I cozied up on the couch, there was no joy to be found. Just a mean little voice singing a self-condemning chorus, full of off-key notes and depressing lyrics:

Yeah, look at all the people who got their act together and sent out cards this year. And this makes the how many-eth year in a row you haven't pulled it off?

Such a lovely family in that one. And look at the matching outfits. And you can't find clean underwear, never mind matching socks, just to get your kids out the door for school.

Check out the porch setup on that card! The family all in their coordinated holiday finery, sitting on the gleaming white steps of their gleaming white Magnolia-Gaines-worthy nouveau farmhouse with the evergreen wreaths symmetrically placed on the double glass doors…while you've displayed this card on a fireplace mantel that oversees a sea of toys and school papers and unfolded laundry and a couch that should have been ditched after college…

Ah, look at that beach shot from so-and-so's anniversary get-away! Look at the pink and peach of the sunset! And when was your last getaway with Ian? To the Dairy Queen after a fight about who had forgotten to sign off on Ben's spelling list.

Yeah.

It was the weirdest thing to be sitting in that room where I regularly encounter joy, only to find myself struggling with thoughts that were anything but joyful. It felt like someone, or something, snuck into my thoughts and stole joy right out from under me.

And, in a very real way, that's exactly what happened. I'd gone into that space with a chip on my shoulder, feeling frazzled and exhausted from life. And while I was in that vulnerable state, a thief slipped through the door.

I believe it was Teddy Roosevelt who said, "Comparison is the thief of joy." And I believe that's true. Comparison invades your heart with sticky fingers, taking anything it deems precious: confidence, peace, contentment—all of it goes in the bag. While you are distracted by other people's shiny things—their clothes, their vacations, their money, their marriages, their perfectly planned Christmas cards—the thief of joy is doing the work of stripping your spirit clean.

> It was the weirdest thing to be sitting in that room where I regularly encounter joy, only to find myself struggling with thoughts that were anything but joyful. It felt like someone, or something, snuck into my thoughts and stole joy right out from under me.

In the cartoons, there's an angel on one shoulder and a devil on the other, and they fight over space in your brain. But with comparison, it feels like there's no angel, only two devils, spewing their hate in surround sound. Whispering in our ear, stealing our joy, and making us feel (and act) crazy.

• • • • • • •

A lot of events led up to that very moment: standing in line at Publix, watching two pecan pies cruise down the conveyor belt in bubbly plastic containers.

No self-respecting Southerner can show up to Thanksgiving without a pie!

I was grasping for straws of justification.

"Paper or plastic?" Checkout Lady asked.

"Plastic is fine," I responded, avoiding eye contact. I just couldn't face the shame.

Contraband in hand, I fled the scene—trashing the receipt on the way out.

It's just one lie. One little pie lie.

• • • • • • •

It all started with a phone call.

My sweet mother-in-law asked what I could bring for Thanksgiving, and I was chomping at the bit. After years on the Thanksgiving sidelines, it was time to make my name in the Backstrom family kitchen.

"I'm bringing a pineapple casserole," I said.

Easy, cheesy, and foolproof. A fantastic choice since I'm the village idiot when it comes to cooking. But no. That wasn't going to be good enough. It was my year to shine, and a casserole just wasn't going to cut it.

"And a pie," I added hastily.

The cartoon devil on my shoulder wrung his hands with glee. His buddy on the other shoulder was delighted. *Boy, this is gonna be good!*

Why did I do it? Because tradition? Because my husband just loves a good pastry? Because of all the things in the world I'm horrible at, baking is #1 on the list? Or is it because I had some of idea of who I should be at this point, some domestic little wife worthy of the Backstrom mantle.

Never mind all that: Holiday magic!!!

My family is Southern, you know. We have generations of cookbooks in our kitchen drawers that serve as proof of our family's excellence. You see, landing your recipe in a Junior League cookbook was like cementing your legacy as a good Southern woman. With scribble-scrawl notes like "shake the egg before cracking it" written in the corners of the pages.

Not only that, but Momma practically raised us on pecan farms. God knows how much of my childhood was spent carrying paper Piggly Wiggly bags around those orchards. We'd stay all day, hunched at the waist, fingers plucking pecan gold from the forest floor, and leave carrying our weight in nuts. Those pecans were parlayed into pastry once deposited in my momma's kitchen. Pies for days. I'm pretty sure my blood type is Karo Syrup.

I was born to cook pecan pie.

So I packed our baby Ben Nugget up in the car and headed

for Momma's house to learn from the master. I had the whole thing planned.

I envisioned Momma whipping up some pastry perfection, the aroma of roasted pecans wafting through the home. Making memories and sipping laughter in our pajamas with Ben Nugget running around the kitchen. We would use Alabama pecans and Granny's recipe. It was gonna be divine.

Problem is, none of that happened. I mean, Ben Nugget probably did run around the kitchen, but as far as pies go… nope. Instead, my mom sold her home and bought a new one—in twenty-four hours. The best-laid plans of mice and men, ya know?

We ended up packing and shopping and eating Mexican during that trip home. It was a grand old time. And before I knew it I was back in Orlando with a sharply dressed toddler, a new pair of jeans…and no stinking pie.

Uh-oh.

So I was entering this Thanksgiving season with plenty of *shoulds* and very little know-how.

Back from Publix, I set the pies on the kitchen table. I couldn't stand to look at them with their little scarlet letters.

But I knew what had to be done. I've seen enough *Criminal Minds* to know that if you are doing the crime, you better be equally committed to the cover-up.

Thus began the process of stripping away their little Publix identities. I scrubbed clean their dirty pasts. No more price tags. No more plastic wrap. No foil pie tins. No, ma'am.

Not for my pies. All the way down to their birthday-suit beginnings, cradled in glass pie dishes. I then rewrapped them in aluminum foil, like they were fresh from my oven.

No time to waste, just hours before Thanksgiving dinner. And as we drove down the interstate I could practically hear my lies screaming out at me from beneath the pineapple casserole.

I walked in the door with my casserole and not one, but two pies. Such an overachiever.

"Oh, MK! I hope it wasn't too much trouble! You didn't have to make two!" my MIL said as she greeted me with a hug.

"She slaved over them all day," snorted the hubs.

I wanted to punch him, but I had to settle for a *You're gonna die for that* grin.

"It wasn't any trouble at all." I smiled, pleased with my not-technically-a-lie response.

"Oh, look at how pretty the crust is! How'd you make it?"

Crap. Crap-crap-crap.

The crime. The cover-up. All of it was perfect.

But I biffed the stinking alibi—rookie mistake! I began to stammer nonsense about cutting butter into the flour but my firstborn saved me.

Thankfully, Ben was elbow-deep in something questionable, so I was able to divert until dinner.

It was dessert time, and I could feel my palms sweating.

"Oh, the pies are wonderful! What's in them?"

"The crust is so flaky! How'd you manage?"

The chandelier felt like a spotlight, illuminating every pore on my face. It felt like the interrogation after a crime. The cops were breaking me down...

"Is this your mom's recipe?"

"Where did you buy the pecans?"

I don't know what made me do it, but the confession flew from my mouth like projectile vomit:

"I didn't make the dadgum pies! They were on sale at Publix."

The first thing I felt was relief, a monkey off my back. But looking around the table at the baffled faces and frozen forks, at three generations of in-laws staring at the lie on their plates...my second emotion took over quickly.

Hot-faced shame.

Ian was giggling so hard I wanted to kill him. My son's namesake and husband's brother, Uncle Ben, just kept eating. It's what he does: diffuse drama by ignoring it. Pap Pap made a comment about how "it's so easy to get a Publix pie, everyone should do it."

But mostly, I wanted to crawl under the table and hide. The rest of the evening was perfectly pleasant. And I made a name for myself in the Backstrom kitchen. The Great Pie Lie is a legacy I will never live down. That whole thing about having your pie and eating it, too? I can tell you, unequivocally, that is garbage.

But it begs the question, doesn't it? Why on earth did I feel like I had to posture myself with a pie? Why not just come in the door, just as I am, declaring that I was Publix and proud?

I'll tell you why: comparison. I was letting the shouts of the devils on my shoulders outrank anything else in my brain. What would have happened if I had just told the truth, that I could barely boil water? What would have happened if I had brought myself to the table instead of some little pie lie?

• • • • • • •

The summer before I entered seventh grade, I decided that I was going to become an astronaut. I had probably just watched *Apollo 13* or something, and the idea of floating around in space and having a hometown elementary school named after me seemed pretty great.

Never mind that I was afraid of heights and hated science. Never mind that all the local elementary schools were named after astronauts who died in space shuttle tragedies, which you'd think might have given me pause. I believed, if I could just keep my eyes on the prize, it was only a matter of time before

> What would have happened if I had brought myself to the table instead of some little pie lie?

I would be leaping around the moon in my pillowy, awesome space suit. I was destined for greatness.

I started an astronaut training regimen. I ordered freeze-dried space-friendly meals from the internet and started jogging a mile every day. I attempted to survive on these meals to prove to myself that I was physically fit for space. After a week, my gums receded, and my body forgot how to poop.

This is fine, I thought. *NASA meals will probably be better, anyways.* And it did seem more efficient to not have to poop in space. For some reason, the box of meals I was consuming as part of my self-inflicted training contained only pineapple fruitcake and strawberry ice cream. But, hey. I wasn't gonna give up just yet. There are no chicken nuggets in space, and I had to be prepared. So I pressed on (occasionally supplementing my astronaut diet with stolen bits of bacon from Momma's cast-iron skillet).

On my first day back at school, I informed the guidance counselor that I would be needing a very "science-focused" seventh-grade curriculum. You know, because career goals.

This was the same guidance counselor I had visited twice the previous year because I almost failed Earth Science. At least she had the good grace not to laugh in my face. Instead, she nodded thoughtfully. "That sounds lovely, Mary Katherine. So, are you going to start paying attention in class now?"

Passive-aggressive much?

I left that meeting with information that proved somewhat problematic to my NASA pursuits. It turned out:

1. Astronauts are actual scientists.
2. Scientists have to go to school for a very, very long time.
3. I had forgotten that I didn't like science…or school.

When my mom picked me up that day, I asked her to take me to McDonald's. Those freeze-dried meals hiding under my bed were dead to me. I had a new dream now, anyways. I was gonna be an FBI agent.

• • • • • • •

An ongoing struggle I have carried into my adult life is this tendency to dream bigger than my abilities (or life circumstances) will ever permit. For instance, whereas a normal person might think, *I have gotten out of shape. I should start to exercise more,* I will sign up for a half-marathon, then buy two boxes of protein smoothies and a hundred-dollar pair of running shoes. Then I might, hypothetically, run six miles the first night, have every muscle in my body cramp up, and text "911—MY LEGS HAVE STOPPED WORKING" to my husband as I lay dying in the yard of one of his coworkers. Hypothetically.

My momma told me I could do anything I set my heart to, and thirty-eight years later, here I am still believing her. Which I guess explains how I found myself at a PTA donut breakfast on my son's first day of school. Now, I will concede that this isn't exactly an "astronaut dream," but it's still a stretch for me. You see, when it comes time to sign up for the school party list, there are two types of parents in this world: those who fight over the baked goodies and those who fight to sign up for paper plates. As we've already established, I don't exactly bake. The truth is, I am very well acquainted with the paper-goods aisle at Publix. So, practically speaking, signing up for PTA was not my smartest move.

But the marathon-running astronaut in me was a believer. And so, there I was. My friend Luis, who has the uncanny ability to make things from Pinterest actually look like things from Pinterest, came along for emotional support and also because he was the one that bribed me into joining PTA in the first place.

"You are gonna do great, MK! What are you even worried about?" he asked. And from his lips to God's ears, I demonstrated exactly what there was to be worried about with a swiftness that impressed even me. It went like this:

The PTA president came and introduced himself to our table, and Luis was all, "Oh, you should definitely tap into MK's amazing social media skills! She's a blogger! Isn't that great?"

PTA President: "Oh, that's wonderful. Are you interested in running our social media?"

Me: "That sounds fun! And I'll be at this school for several years because I have another kid coming down the hatch!"

The PTA president squirmed. "I'm sorry, did you say... hatch?"

Me: "OMG! I meant, like, preschool. Not like (motioning toward my lady bits) an actual HATCH. Oh, goodness! I'm sorry! Holy smokes, you thought I was talking about—"

I got a kick under the table from Luis, which I took as a strong suggestion to stop talking. The PTA president smiled warmly and exited our company, and I turned to scowl at Luis.

"See, this is why I sign up for paper plates!" I hissed.

"You are doing great," Luis whispered. "Less is more. Less is more."

Bottom line, there are some people in this world whom God has gifted with a specific set of skills. Skills like baking, fund-raising, craft making, and showing up to places on time. Let's call these humans the "Pinterest People." Like Luis.

Then, there are people who fight for the opportunity to bring paper plates to the party—or even better, to write a check. Generally speaking, these are the parents who forget the day of the class party until right at morning drop-off, then— *oh crap!*—they have to run to Publix and grab some paper plates before eleven o'clock. They are the "Paper Plate People."

As I sat through the rest of that PTA meeting with my Pinterest dad friend, Luis, it occurred to me that attempting to become a bona fide PTA parent was going to feel about as natural as eating freeze-dried pineapple fruitcake and running several miles a day. I might survive the ordeal with receding gums and epic constipation, but to what end? This was clearly not a good fit for me, no matter how badly I wanted it to work.

Isn't it ironic how our aspirational efforts can cause so much frustration and self-loathing? It reminds me of those annoying iPhone upgrades that nobody wanted or asked for. It takes so much time to upgrade, and when it's finally finished, we no longer recognize the internet. What was wrong with the last iOS? At what point do we get to just...*be*?

I wasn't born to be a Pinterest Person. No matter how much I wish I could upgrade myself into a mom that makes cotton-ball snowmen, in the end my Christmas craft will resemble some horrific, melty version of a rabid polar bear.

Deep in my bones, I know that I'm a Paper Plate Person. But I have this unsettling feeling that my role is not enough. That maybe, just maybe, the better parents are the ones who can craft snowmen out of cotton balls. But not everybody can be crafty, and you know what? Cupcakes need to be served on something. Kool-Aid needs to go in a cup. And when Johnny has icing all over his mouth, his teacher is going to reach for a napkin.

How did all those paper goods make their way into the classroom? The Paper Plate Parent did that, thank you very much.

But still, a voice remains in the rafters of my mind, criticizing my every move. That devil on the shoulder that I can't quite flick away—it whispers that I am failing. That I should do more, become more, be more.

Reach for the stars; become an astronaut. Get their attention; become a rock star. You can be anything; run for president. And if you reach thirty-something and haven't achieved any of that? Well for goodness' sake, you do-nothing putz, at least join the PTA!

• • • • • • •

When my son was about eighteen months old, I bought this adorable wooden toy I remembered having as a child. It was simple: a block of wood with shapes cut out of it. There was a star-shaped hole, a circle-shaped hole, and a square-shaped hole...you get the point. Then there were little blocks that filled the shapes of the holes. And a hammer, because why not? Toddlers love hammers.

I remember sitting on the couch, watching my little boy wrestle with the yellow star-shaped block. He wanted it to go through the circle-shaped hole, but no amount of hammering or growling or whining was making that happen for him. He hammered and hammered and whined and finally picked up the toy and threw it across the room.

In that moment, an ideal parent would have walked across the room and knelt to meet their child's eyes. An ideal parent would have said, "Sweetie, you can't fling blocks across the room because you are feeling mad."

But we've already established that I'm not ideal, so let me tell you what I did. I went to my son, I scooped him up in my arms, and I held him as he cried. I didn't think that Ben needed a lesson in shapes or a lecture on patience. He needed comfort while negotiating the heartbreaking physics of star blocks and square-shaped holes.

For the last thirty-eight years, I've been trying to find my place in this world—but that ever-elusive star-shaped hole just doesn't seem to exist. I have chased having the perfect job, the perfect body, the perfect life, and being the perfect spouse, and after failing to achieve any of those things, I believed the failure was mine. My edges were just too wonky. I was too much here, and not enough there. Too ADHD to complete my college degree, not conservative enough to speak at that church. Too scatterbrained for PTA, not educated enough for that job. And it's not like I wasn't trying.

Every day, I brought my best and tried my hardest, but the life I imagined—the one where everything would fall neatly into place—never materialized. No matter how hard I tried, or hammered, or screamed at it to make it work. I felt exhausted from the effort of just being alive.

Where the hell was my star-shaped hole?

· ·

TOUR GUIDE TAKEAWAYS

- When comparison comes knocking at my door, I almost always answer. That's how I end up in such ridiculous hijinks (pie duplicity, overtalking at PTA meetings, etc.). My abject panic in the face of comparison knows no bounds. What is the funniest thing you've done in the name of comparison?

- And now let's take it down a notch. What's the saddest thing you've done in the name of comparison?

- Fill in the blanks:
    - I'm too much _____.

    - I'm not enough_____.

· ·

CHAPTER 9

KING OF THE GOBLINS

So, the Labyrinth is a piece of cake, is it?
Well, let's see how you deal
with this little slice.
—Jareth, *Labyrinth*

If there's such a thing as death by a thousand cuts, I can't help but think this is how joy dies. With the daily cuts of comparison, attacking us repeatedly.

I recently read an article written by two NIH (National Institutes of Health) scientists, in which they published their findings on a fascinating study identifying patterns of thought. Participants were randomly prompted throughout the day to record thought samples using palmtop computers that they carried for two weeks. The findings were incredible. When the data was compiled and categorized, comparative thought accounted for 12 percent of all thoughts the participants logged. These findings reveal just how loud the voices of those little devils can be.

I wonder, What does this do to our souls? This lo-fi comparison background drone that accompanies so much of our day? What if we thumped those devil DJs off our shoulders, and allowed our brains to breathe?

What if we said, "I am not a PTA mom, and that's okay. More than okay—it's part of what makes me special. I am not less than; I'm a different shape. And that's how God created me."

What if we said, "I can't make pies from scratch. The truth is I make mac and cheese in the microwave. But I love pie, and I'm more than happy to find the best one that Publix has ever made."

What would a little self-compassion look like? That gentle assessment of who you are and that loving acceptance of the truth? I'll tell you right now, it would be revolutionary. It would restore the joy in your soul.

There is only one you in the whole wide world. When you try to be something or somebody you're not, you're depriving yourself of the joy that comes

> What would a little self-compassion look like? That gentle assessment of who you are and that loving acceptance of the truth?

with knowing who you truly are. And not only that, you're depriving the world of the joy that comes with getting to know the real you. If we were all a bunch of square-shaped pegs running around in this world, well, the world would start to look pretty dang square. Those edges that make it hard to fit in are the same edges that make you a star. God knit you together while you were still in the womb, and those quirks are there by design. Believe me, the things that make you weird are exactly what makes you wonderful.

Not that I'm out here in the world rocking my edges with pride. The truth is, comparison still has a foothold in my life, and it's actively stealing my joy. Those little devils have made themselves comfy on my shoulders, snuggled up cozy to my ears with a direct line of self-doubt dialed straight into my head. But I'm telling you, therapy has helped immensely to stop their toxic influence. Slowly but surely, I'm replacing these thoughts with affirming and life-giving narratives. They're still on my shoulders, but the eviction has been served.

I'm trying, friends. I'm trying.

• • • • • • •

I met a girl at a conference last weekend. Funniest girl I've ever met. So I tried to be hilarious, too. And it made me feel tired.

I saw a mom at my son's preschool yesterday. She packed

her kids healthy lunches, and they actually freaking ate them. So last night I tried to force-feed my kids carrots and meat loaf, and they cried.

That made me feel like a failure.

There's a girl I follow on Instagram. I've known her for years, and she's lost over sixty pounds and jumps up and down in her bikini without feeling mortified. That's basically a superpower in my mind, because when I sit down in the shower, I feel like the Michelin Tire Man. There is NO jumping. I want my curvy body to just disappear.

The mean things I say to myself are effective. They make me feel disgusting.

I have a friend who makes viral videos. I love making videos, but mine don't have as much success. Sometimes I wonder if what I publish is embarrassing and stupid.

That shame makes me want to stop creating.

Unsurprisingly, I go to therapy. A lot. Partly, because I'm a hot mess. And partly because I love to talk and it's nice to have this person who is basically a paid hostage listen for an entire hour without acting bored.

Usually, my therapist nods his head and says "mhm" or asks me probing questions. But this particular week, my therapist sat back quietly until the hour was done.

I told him about lunch-box anxiety, and Michelin tire fat rolls, and my stupid, stupid videos. When I was done, he leaned forward and raised an eyebrow.

"You are such a kind person, MK. You seem to really love your friends and believe in what they do. You celebrate their joy."

I puffed up a little. It's nice when someone sees goodness in you.

But he continued, "So why are you so hateful to yourself?"

"Oh, hell," I muttered before folding over in sobs.

He wasn't wrong. I am my own worst bully. The things I say to myself are plain awful. I would never say such things to anyone I loved. Honestly, I wouldn't even say them to anyone I *didn't* love.

And why do I do this? All I know is that I go WAY out of my way to talk down to myself so that I never feel too much pride or experience too much joy.

Turns out, joy is a scary feeling. When we find ourselves in a moment so happy and beautiful, the only thing our brains know how to do is prepare us for the crash landing.

> Turns out, joy is a scary feeling. When we find ourselves in a moment so happy and beautiful, the only thing our brains know how to do is prepare us for the crash landing.

When we start feeling proud of ourselves or enjoying a special moment, we start to ask:

What could go wrong? How will this get messed up? What is the worst possible outcome of this wonderful scenario?

We celebrate our friends' lives so selflessly because their joy isn't a risk to us. It isn't SCARY.

But we talk down to ourselves because OUR joy is downright terrifying.

I mean, what would happen if we believed we were beautiful? What would happen if we celebrated our OWN talents? If we loved our bodies and our minds? If we allowed ourselves to fly?

Well, sometimes things that fly, fall. And that hurts like hell. So, I guess that's what could happen.

Maybe that's why, instead of letting ourselves take the risk to be joyful, we say, *Nope. You stay put. Right there. Where it's miserably safe. If you already believe you are a failure, then failure doesn't hurt, now does it?*

I left therapy this week and did something pretty badass. I challenge you to do the same.

I made a new friend.

Her name is Mary Katherine, and she's pretty freaking cool. She has a beautiful smile and an understated wit. Her jokes are awkward, but that is pretty dang endearing. She's an amazing person, if I must say so.

I'm learning to like her a little bit. Maybe one day, if I work hard enough, she'll feel loved.

• • • • • • •

One of my favorite movies of all time is a Jim Henson musical called *Labyrinth*. It's not just quirky, I'll tell you right now: This movie is downright weird. The plot centers around a girl named Sarah, who at the beginning of the movie is furious that her parents are going on a date, because that means she's being forced to stay home and babysit her baby brother, Toby. Toby is a baby, so he cries, and this pushes Sarah over the teenage hormonal edge. She announces that she wishes the goblins would take her brother away, and with that she flips off the light switch and shuts the nursery door. And that's when things get creepy, honestly. The moment the door closes, her brother stops crying, and the house grows dead silent. Well, guess who was listening when she cast that irresponsible wish? The Goblin King himself, y'all. David Bowie in spandex. I told you this movie was great.

To Sarah's great shock, the Goblin King has taken Toby and is holding him captive in his castle, which is surrounded by a great, twisting Labyrinth. He gives Sarah thirteen hours to solve the Labyrinth before her brother becomes a goblin, and that's the gist of the rest of the movie. Sister trying to save brother.

There are so many weird and wonderful scenes that take place in this movie, but I do have a favorite. Sarah is desperately racing against time, trying to save her brother, when Jareth (the Goblin King) pops in and asks her if she's enjoying his Labyrinth. Sarah is snarky and says that it isn't so hard, and right before Jareth leaves, he points his finger toward a clock on the wall and mimics a winding motion. Sarah is outraged that an hour has disappeared when she thought she would have thirteen.

"That's not fair!" she objects.

The Goblin King smirks.

"You say that so often. I wonder what your basis for comparison is."

• • • • • • •

The funny thing about this comparison trap is the standards keep evolving. What was considered beautiful or successful or valiant a generation ago doesn't quite measure up today.

If my husband challenged somebody to a duel for my honor, I would not at all be impressed. I would be pissed because duels are stupid. But have they always been seen that way?

And sometimes I wish I could live in ancient Rome, when the ideal body type looked pillowy like mine. I've lived through the heroin chic '90s and the tanning bed 2000s. And now I'm doing my best to love my body in this nip-tuck Kardashian era. It's exhausting, and discouraging, and sometimes I just want to throw my hands up in the air and yell because it's not fair!

But what is my basis for comparison, y'all? What is it for any of us? The standards are always changing, which means they ain't all they're cracked up to be.

When this generation passes the baton…and it will, willingly or not…a new measure of perfection will rise. Who knows what that will look like.

Maybe a body type like mine will be the new sexy. Maybe it won't.

Maybe a mom style like mine will be the new standard. Maybe it won't.

Maybe a home decorated like mine or a marriage like mine or a life like mine will be the goal of that next generation. Or maybe none of it will.

And at that point…who cares? Why am I aiming for a target that shape-shifts on the daily? And why am I letting anyone besides myself dictate what my target is? It feels like that panic attack I had playing *Duck Hunt* back in the '80s. Getting a cramp in my trigger finger while the ducks just keep on flying. The target will move, and then it will move again. And that's the way of this world. So, we really have two choices. We can drive ourselves crazy trying to keep up with the ducks, or, hear me out…we could just stop.

We are handcrafted by God to be unique, so what is our basis of comparison?

There is only one you. This one. Today. Not you from the past. Not you that will be. This girl. Now. This moment. This breath. This beat.

• • • • • • •

The other day I picked up my Bible to revisit the story of Samson. It's a tale I heard a million times as a child, but I'd never read it myself. Everything I knew about this Hulk-like hero came from illustrated posters. I remember our Sunday school teacher would sit in the middle of the room, shuffling through her pictures, while we filled our bellies with Goldfish crackers and juice and listened to the drama unfold.

What I remember most about Samson are his ginormous muscles and his Fabio-level hair. He looked like He-Man, Master of the Universe (if He-Man had a naughty, cute girlfriend).

Of course, every superhero has a flaw in their armor, a weak spot that can make them vulnerable. For Samson, it was his long, gorgeous hair. God had forbidden Samson to cut it. If he did, he would lose his powers.

Enter Delilah, with her cute gold earrings and sexy purple maxi dress. I remember thinking she looked like my mom, and wishing I had her outfit. But Delilah was a sneaky one, from enemy

There is only one you. This one. Today. Not you from the past. Not you that will be. This girl. Now. This moment. This breath. This beat.

lines, and she had ulterior motives. She snuggled up close to our He-Man hero, hoping to find his weakness. Well, Samson was really a fan of that dress, because he straight up spilled the beans. And what happened next wasn't surprising: He got a very bad haircut.

Delilah waited for Samson to fall asleep and then, in a classic mean-girl-at-the-slumber-party move, she took some scissors to his hair. He woke up with a mullet, got thrown into prison, and, I assume, was too weak to break free of his chains. On top of all that, he was dumped by his girlfriend. Talk about a terrible day. All in all, it was a pretty rad story for the preschool kids at Noah's Nursery.

Of course, we were given the G-rated version. The story was much, much worse. Not only did Samson get thrown into prison, but he was abandoned by the Spirit of God, and felt deeply and utterly alone. As if all that weren't terrible enough, his eyes were gouged out and he was paraded around town with no eyeballs, being mocked by his enemies. Samson eventually redeemed his story, in a depressing kind of way. With one last dose of miraculous strength, he collapsed the enemy's temple, killing everyone inside, including our hero, Samson. I imagine that image wouldn't play too well on a Sunday school illustration poster.

But what struck me most when reading this story as an adult was this: It wasn't the haircut that killed him. Samson lost so much more to Delilah than a few little clips of his mane. He lost his purpose. His God-given path. He lost who he was born to be.

You see, Samson was to be a Nazirite from birth. In ancient Israel there was a special group of people who took a vow of dedication to God. And with that vow came some restrictions: abstaining from wine, avoiding dead bodies (excuse me, what?), and also, not cutting your hair. This vow was what brought Samson closer to God, and it was the source of his strength. By revealing his covenant with God to Delilah, he'd betrayed his Nazirite vow. The downfall of Sampson didn't start with a haircut...it started long before that. It started the moment he lost sight of his birthright, the person God made him to be.

• • • • • • •

Nehemiah 8:10 says, "The joy of the LORD is your strength." Friends, do you know what this means? It means we are like Samson. We have special powers—and those powers are born out of joy. Sometimes I wonder what Delilah said that convinced Samson he wasn't enough. How many lies did he buy into before he ultimately lost his way?

• • • • • • •

If we want to protect our joy—our *strength*—then there's something we have to remember: The thief of comparison is a masterful liar. Her whispers feel warm and sexy. A thief doesn't announce their presence or bust in with guns a-blazing. They sneak through the door, as quiet as a whisper, before stealing away with our joy.

Look at the places in your life where comparison steals your joy. Study the source of those sexy voices that whisper, "You're not enough." Then ask yourself: *Where are they coming from?*

Social media? That gossipy friend from work? A show that you watch on TV? If that's the case, delete Instagram. Find a different break room for lunch. Turn off that show that makes you want to grab blankets to cover your stomach.

I'm not saying you're gonna lose your eyeballs or get crushed in an enemy temple, but isn't the thought of losing your joy devastating enough on its own? It's time that we stop returning to places and people that wield scissors against our joy.

Joy is more powerful, more precious, more necessary than any of us ever realized. And the only way to shake those devils off your shoulders is to reject their narrative altogether. You are a unique creation, with a unique purpose. A one-in-billions creation. For all of his flaws, the Goblin King, Jareth, was right about one little thing: There is no basis of comparison. There has not been, and there never will be, another version of you.

Isn't it time that you and I stop taking advice from thieves?

- -

TOUR GUIDE TAKEAWAYS

- Where do the voices that steal your joy come from? Or as Jareth (the Goblin King) would ask: What is your basis for comparison?

- Somehow, we've got to be both humble enough to receive feedback and wise enough to have gate controls over who gets into the precious property of our hearts. Let me ask you this: Do you allow just anyone to speak into your life? Or are you selective with the people who speak into your life?

- -

CHAPTER 10

TINFOIL HATS

You're the strangest person I ever met,
she said & I said you too & we decided
we'd know each other a long time.
—Brian Andreas

Remember those Great Depression–era scientists who studied what makes people happy? Do you remember what the study revealed was the single most important factor when it came to a joyful life? Don't worry. This isn't a pop quiz. The answer is *community*. The study participants who lived the happiest lives weren't the richest, or the most attractive, or the most successful in their careers. They were the ones who loved their friends and family well, and, in turn, felt well-loved. Community isn't made on the couch in pajamas, watching *The Office* for the fiftieth time. It's found by opening our hearts to others and allowing them into our lives.

I know it's scary to let people in, and we've all been burned before. But crazy joy requires peopling. That's a scientific fact. Joy requires risking your heart on friendship, over and over again. The good news is, you can always go back to the couch once you've found your people. The only thing better than binge-watching Netflix on the couch in your pajamas is binge-watching Netflix on the couch in your pajamas with the people who love you most. Take it from me. I know.

One of my best friends, Meredith, is obsessed with murder shows. It's freaking hilarious, too, because she's this precious, gentle lady from Utah who has three kids and drives a Honda. Mer will seriously whip up some homemade muffins, snuggle up on the couch with a warm blanket, and binge-watch serial killers with the same casual comfort that my mom has watching *Property Brothers*.

It's always a blast watching murder shows with Mer because she hasn't just seen the episodes—she's done the deep-dive supplemental research, too: journalistic articles, podcast episodes, Reddit threads, you name it. She won't put on something random and unvetted. It's going to be a high-quality docuseries from the Now That's What I Call a Body Count collection. We're not just *watching* a Ted Kaczynski documentary. We're taking a guided Jeep ride through the savanna with a driver who knows all the wildlife. Except Mer is the tour guide, and we're learning about the Unabomber. I'm telling you, never a dull moment.

And while I've been known to binge-watch a *Snapped*

season or two, I prefer a different brand of dark, rabbit-hole escapism. It's not the murder shows or the cult shows that suck me in. No. I love a good conspiracy theory. Now hear me out, I'm not twisting up tinfoil hats or stockpiling my basement with beans. I like researching conspiracy theories because they're like these odd little mental puzzles. They force me to climb into these wacky little boxes that I have to logic myself out of. It's like solving a murder but with a lot less blood, and in the end, you know all there is to know about the moon landing.

For instance: flat-earthers. I admit, when I first realized that "flat earth" was trending, I figured it was a satire of conspiracy. Because, surely, there is nobody in this day and age who thinks we live on an ecological pancake. But oh, they do.

Jumping into that rabbit hole, I'll tell you what I found. A bunch of outlandish theories, which made me raise my eyebrows—and some astoundingly beautiful science. It doesn't take much, just a quick Google search of "prove that the earth isn't flat," and a wealth of peer-reviewed data appears: articles, scientific journals, and firsthand reports from astronauts. The evidence piles up against this flat-earth theory and squashes it like a pancake (heh).

But flat-earthers will not go quietly into the night, and I think I've figured out why. Because central to this movement is the absurd belief that planet Earth is the center of the universe. Honestly, the audacity is impressive.

Now, when I tell you I love conspiracies because I get to

know more about something—this is exactly what I mean. Let me tell you some crazy things that I learned would happen if the earth was shaped like a Frisbee. For one thing, gravity would go haywire and push things toward the center of the planet. This would include water, which would get sucked to the middle of the Frisbee to create a ginormous, brackish pool. There would be no tectonic movement, so mountains and canyons are out. Plants and trees would grow diagonally since they develop in the opposite direction of gravity's pull. But the truth is that no vegetation would survive (or anything else for that matter). You see, the core of our planet creates its magnetic field, and absent a magnetic field, charged particles from the sun would strip away the earth's atmosphere. The air and oceans would escape into space and we'd all be cooked up like bacon. You have to admit that it's funny: When you put yourself at the center of the universe, everything else stops working.

• • • • • • •

I remember graduation day like it was yesterday. I can see us snapping pictures in our gowns. The celebratory throwing of our caps. Green Day's "Time of Your Life" playing through the speakers as a slideshow with four years of memories flashed before our eyes. I recall the crying, the hugging, the swearing that we would all "keep in touch" and that things would never, ever change between us.

"Friends are forever!" we proclaimed. "We will never change!"

Our pink friendship bracelets were tied about our wrists, symbolizing our commitment.

Twenty years later, my faded pink bracelet has retired to a trunk in my closet, where it rests with hundreds of photographs, notes, and letters from the early 2000s.

Those friends? Well, I haven't seen them in years. We've loosely stayed in touch, thanks to social media, but we all have very different lives. And honestly, that's okay. I hold nothing but love for those wonderful women. We are still friends, but our paths have drifted apart.

It isn't sad. It isn't a tragedy. It just *is*.

I've been alive long enough to earn a few gray hairs, and this is what I've learned about relationships: You can count on one hand the number of friends you will keep through significant life transitions. When you graduate college, friends will drop off the radar. Keep in mind, they are not fleeing the radar. When you marry, a few more friends will drift away. And we all know what happens when you have children. It's a natural part of relationships, this drifting apart.

People grow as individuals, and our lives take different directions. It took a whole lot of therapy to make peace with this fact, but I'm here now, so let me share what I've learned. Perspective changes everything. Where you stand, and the angle from which you view things, can alter your entire experience. If you've ever accidentally opened the forward-facing camera on your phone and looked down in horror to see that you kinda look like Ursula rising up out of the sea...well, then you know what I'm talking about.

If you want to have joy, deep joy, in friendship—then perspective is of paramount importance.

• • • • • • •

When my son was about six months old, we played peekaboo every morning in his high chair. The look of genuine surprise when he uncovered his face—it was like he couldn't believe I was still there. I'll never forget how his laughter bubbled up to the ceiling, or the sparkle of light in his eyes. I don't care how much he loves Roblox these days—nothing compares to that peekaboo grin.

The thing is, babies love peekaboo because they're learning something about the world. That when something disappears, it isn't necessarily gone. This is known as object permanence. My son is eight years old now, and we don't play peekaboo anymore. Benjamin knows that when I leave the room, or the house, or even the state—I continue to exist. This doesn't mean that my kids don't care when I leave, but they're able to let me go. Because ultimately, they know that I'm going to come back.

Momma's gone, but not gone *forever*.

• • • • • • •

I was eight years old when I developed my very first conspiracy theory. There were a few extenuating circumstances that I believe fed into my beliefs. One, I was bored. I'd been stuck inside for almost four days, during the blizzard of 1993. For context, a blizzard in Alabama means more than two inches of snow. Still, our electricity was out and everything was cold and dark and boring. I hopped in my bed under the covers and *pop!* A little buzz of static electricity discharged on my finger. Perhaps it wouldn't have shocked me so much if I hadn't seen the actual spark. But the little flash-bang of my finger on the blanket struck me as highly unusual, so I ran to my momma and informed her that my blanket had zapped me. She reminded me that static electricity was a thing and told me to play with my brother.

Later that day, back in my room, I felt another pop. Now I was convinced something was amiss. I'd had plenty of static pops before, but never two in the same spot in the same day. I started theorizing about what, if anything, could cause this mysterious increase in charges. Was it the snowstorm? Or had I recently developed some power? The second theory made me feel more like an X-Man, so I decided to run with it. I walked around my room, eyeing the blanket, rubbing my hands together. I needed to practice building up my charge so I could learn to control my powers. I spent an hour or so in my bedroom, pacing back and forth, rubbing my hands, and popping my blanket. With every discharge that popped on that blanket, I was affirmed in my magical hypothesis. I felt certain that any moment, Charles Xavier would knock on our front door and inform my family that I was quite special, and I needed to leave Dothan, Alabama, for training. There was a clear and consistent pattern to my powers. Albeit only during a one-off blizzard with the power out.

The funny thing is, this ability to see patterns is a fine-tuned survival instinct. Our ancestors used this mental exercise to protect themselves from predators. If two of their cave-buddies ate berries and died the next day, well, they'd probably stop eating those berries. If the woods went silent and the birds flew away, they'd crouch down and look for a predator, since the last time this happened some saber-toothed something took out Uncle Grunt.

But that very same tendency can go haywire in our brains, creating nonexistent links between cause and effect. The blanket zaps me; I have superpowers. The blanket zaps me in the winter; the snow brought me superpowers. This obviously makes me a snow-charged X-Woman who is in the early stages of discovering her power.

Something else happens with conspiracy theories. We take all the data we see around us and bend it to fit our narrative, filtering every piece of information through the same biased lens. We also seek out agreeing opinions because we want to believe we are right. This confirmation bias brings us one step closer to making a tinfoil hat.

I told my little brother about my magical powers, and he enthusiastically agreed it was possible. So then I trained in his room, pacing the floor, rubbing my hands, and creating static pops on his quilt. We were ecstatic to see our narrative coming to life—so much so that he decided to test his own powers. And wouldn't you know, when he paced the room and rubbed his hands together, he was able to discharge static, too. Did this disprove my theory that I had special powers? Uh, no. It just made them genetic. And now there were two X-Men in our house, refining their electrical powers.

Sadly, the snow melted, and the weather warmed up, the power came back on, and our snow-charged powers went away. We contemplated what would happen if we moved up north, but Momma was having none of it. For some reason, she was convinced that it was our fuzzy socks on the rugs and the many quilts for the cold weather combined that made our home so electrical. Too bad Momma didn't get it. She was probably just jealous.

Poor Momma didn't have any powers.

• • • • • • •

My best friends live in four different states, and I rarely get to see them in person. We are all on these individual journeys around the sun, and I admit I miss them a lot.

There are days when I'd love nothing more than to crash on Mer's couch and binge-watch some murder shows. But she lives in Utah and I'm in Alabama. And the thing is, I understand object permanence. Mer's way over in Utah, but our friendship is not gone. I can pick up the phone and call her anytime I want. There are weeks when we speak almost every day. Then we can go weeks without so much as a meme texted between us. These periods of absence don't mean our friendship is going through a rough patch or our bond isn't strong. To the contrary, it's just as strong as ever and neither of us doubts that. Time passes but love remains.

When we apply the concept of object permanence to friendship, community starts to feel less fragile. Instead of buying into the theory that friendship dies, you can see things from a different perspective: that, like planets, we each are on our own journey around the sun, and sometimes our paths cross and our worlds overlap, and sometimes we feel further away. It's a natural progression of human relationships, this coming and going from orbit.

Like one of your bridesmaids that you haven't spoken to in years—the distance is rarely because she just stopped being your friend. You two were college besties who wore each other's clothes to your favorite bar on Thursdays. The two of you burned slice-and-bake cookies in your shoddy apartment oven during that snowstorm. She stood up with you while you exchanged vows with the love of your life. And over time, you both evolved, like anything alive and thriving tends to do.

The things that made your bond so strong, like the fun

of getting ready together in the same toothpaste-splattered mirror or planning your spring break road trips, aren't priorities in either of your lives anymore. But you're still happy for her when a picture of her adorable family pops up on your Instagram feed. And she still laughed and thought of you when she finally parted with the ratty old slippers you always teased her for putting on whenever she walked in the door.

I'm not going to deny that community is hard: There's an ache in each of us, longing for connection, that we desperately want to resolve. And when we try, and fail, to establish new relationships, we feel that ache even more acutely.

It is human nature to avoid discomfort—so you start looking for patterns, trying to find some cause for this ache that you feel in the center of your heart. You remember all the relationships in your past that were formed, cherished, and eventually fizzled. And perhaps, in the depths of your loneliness, you might decide community is just too hard. That building friendships is too high-risk, and too painful to continue pursuing.

You want to protect yourself from the hurt of lost relationships, or the ache of not having any at all. So, you shut down your heart, and say, "This is too hard," and think perhaps you are better off solo.

The thing is, this instinct to self-preserve has the potential to go haywire. Sometimes our caveman brains forget that discomfort can be a good thing. Take hunger, for example.

It's not a pleasant feeling. So, what if we could eliminate hunger—would that eliminate our need for food? Or would we simply lose the sensation of discomfort while our bodies slowly starved?

The discomfort of hunger literally keeps us alive, because it keeps us looking for food. Food is a necessity of life, even when it hurts us. A bout of food poisoning is certainly not proof that food should be eliminated from life. We know this is true, but when it comes to community…we struggle applying the same concept.

The ache for community, and longing for friendship, missing the people you love—all of this is physiological proof that you literally *need* community. Like food brings nourishment to our bodies, community is nourishment for our souls. That's why we long for it on such a deep level. And when we find it, we want it to last, and are devastated when it doesn't.

Here's the thing: Anything seasoned with joy will taste bittersweet, because we want it to last forever. Remember that joy longs for eternity, deep eternity. And that's what community is.

A joy worth pursuing, worth aching for, worth losing and finding again.

> Remember that joy longs for eternity, deep eternity. And that's what community is. A joy worth pursuing, worth aching for, worth losing and finding again.

• • • • • • •

All of this to say, I am in no way an expert on friendship. In fact, I'll take that one step further and admit: It's a place where I struggle. I do my best to nourish these precious relationships, both those in my immediate vicinity and those held together through cell towers. But the truth is, sometimes I mess things up. I'm an imperfect person loving imperfect people; our community is going to get messy. Which is why my friends and I stock up on grace and do our best to release expectations.

You wanna talk about something that should have its own murder show, it's that nefarious little word: *expectations*. How many relationships fall apart over unreasonable or unmet expectations? I can tell you in my own life story it amounts to a significant body count. Because it's the thing that can kill relationships with a slow drop of poison administered stealthily over time. We expect our friends to know how to show up. We expect them to know the right things to say and how to avoid the wrong things. We craft a definition of support from a friend to mean always taking our side and never disagreeing with us. We have an expectation of friendship that says there's room for challenge…but we don't really mean it. We want all smooth sailing, and when it doesn't go that way, we'll dramatically declare, the back of our hand flipped to our fainting forehead, that we should have *known* that things wouldn't turn out the way we thought.

But life doesn't play that way, does it? And that means friendships don't, either.

What are the expectations you have of your friends? What are the expectations you have of yourself as a friend, as a community member? Does it leave room for life to happen, for a few weeks to go by where you're running busy or your friend is, and it doesn't mean the end of all things?

If you want to keep joy in your friendships, the ones that are healthy and life-giving, the first thing to do is show unhelpful expectations the door. Otherwise, they'll sit hunched in the corner of your mind, like some creepy little goblin of joy, whispering raspy commentary that tears your community apart: *They don't really love you; you aren't lovable; you'd be better off alone.*

The truth is, there is literally no such thing as "better off alone." Body, mind, and soul, you are constructed for connection—which is why you ache when it's missing.

· · · · · · ·

Have you ever heard the saying "Even a broken clock is right twice a day"? It means even the most unreliable of sources can be right on certain occasions. And after serious consideration, I've decided that's the case with those flat-earth conspiracy theorists. Because of all the quirky, deluded communities that this digital age has brought forth, from Pizzagate to JFK truthers to Area 51 stormers, the flat-earthers have something that is distinctive and special. They've built their community on their real-world perspective (however flawed it may be).

"Just look outside! It's flat—not curved!? How are we the only ones who can see this?" They aren't crazy, the rest of us are, and that's their common ground. They've linked arms, named their cause, and found people. Good for them, right?

It's not a community you and I would find much joy in (though I do want one of their T-shirts). But dang it, if this doesn't drive home the point that there's a lid for every pot. There's a group of friends for everyone, even those who believe that the earth is shaped like a Frisbee. If there's a community that can congregate over that, then I'm certain there's community for everyone.

I mean, everyone. Those who are still making their way in the world, asking questions, figuring out their relationship with God, mothering with heart and imperfection, trying to make their marriage work, juggling work and school. I want that kind of joy for you, just like I do for myself.

And the speed bump we keep encountering on the way are these lies we keep telling ourselves: that we are not smart or fun, that we are unlovable and there isn't a place for us in the world.

And just like any conspiracy theorist would, we take that belief and bend everything else to support it. We take every insecurity, every shortcoming, and use it as evidence to explain our feelings of scarcity. But we're looking at ourselves with a deeply flawed, incredibly magnified lens. If we take a step back, if we broaden our perspective…things start to look a bit different. I mean, goodness, if your backyard is the only thing you see, it's reasonable to think the world is flat. But there's a world that exists outside the circular lens of that magnifying glass. A big, round world, full of community, just waiting to be discovered.

And maybe you're having a difficult time. I understand, I've been there, too. But there's no way God made this big, round world and left you and me on it, alone.

There's something you need to remember about this journey to relationship joy. There are times when your path takes you closer to the sun, and there are times when you move further away. It's part of this journey around the sun, these changes and comings and goings. Winters are hard, but they don't last forever. That's the beauty of seasons. Eventually, your orbit will cross someone else's, and you'll remember the warmth of the sun.

Spring will come, and so will community. I promise, you'll find your people. But it's going to take effort, and it's going to get awkward. You will have times when your efforts leave you exhausted, or embarrassed, and wanting to quit. You'll feel tempted to chuck this whole community thing, and believe me, I understand. On more than one occasion I've imagined my life as a cheeseaholic cat lady hermit. I've found myself low in the pits of social despair, and I've thrown my hands up in the air.

"Forget this. I quit. I'm going to bed. I'll order Taco Bell for the rest of my life and adopt a few hundred cats."

I even dabbled in this life for about twenty-four hours and let me tell you what it got me. A bad case of heartburn, and more poop to scoop. Don't get me wrong, I love my cats. Chicken and Waffles are great. But they don't fill the spiritual, biological, or mental need that I have for human connection.

Which means, even when things are hard, and we want to quit, you and me, we have to keep showing up.

When those girls at the MOPS table are cliquey and rude, we have to keep showing up.

When relationships break, we take the time to heal and then we have to keep showing up.

When fear gets in our way like an untied shoelace, we have to keep showing up.

When we show up to a small group and verbally vomit about talking beavers, yes. Even then. Keep showing up.

And I love people, I do. But for just a moment, hear me out. Community isn't just about people. It's about you. Your need to be encouraged, uplifted, challenged. Your need to laugh at jokes. Your need to have a soft landing place when life gets hard. Your need to love and be loved in return. These things are so important.

So when it's hard to show up for the sake of others, do me a favor: Love yourself enough to acknowledge your needs and love yourself enough to meet them.

Show up. Even when people are...well, you know, peopley, and community is scary, and you're afraid of getting burned. *Show up.*

You can't pour from an empty cup; you absolutely need community. And when you let other people pour into your cup, you'll be surprised how fast it fills up. And when that cup is overflowing with love, and you're passing that love all around, the craziest thing will happen. Despite all your fears and misgivings and doubts...when you build community, when you show up for yourself, and when you show up for others...

Crazy joy shows up, too.

TOUR GUIDE TAKEAWAYS

- I'm of the solid belief that you can't have joy, not crazy joy, without community. I know people who are trying to do this joy thing solo, shielding themselves from other people. But here's what I've figured out: The sneeze guards at the buffet of friendship don't do a whole lot. Community is what matures our joy and pulls us away from making joy our own selfish fiefdom. Community takes joy and shows us how to apply it. And joy applied, multiplies. Where have you been protecting yourself when it comes to building community? Have you found your people? If not, what are you waiting on?

- I'm on the path to accepting that we somehow have to stay flexible *and* smart when it comes to operating in community. For me, that looks like this: I'm gonna let you show me who you are. I'm going to believe you. I'm going to do my darndest to not write you a pre-script, and also not rewrite the script you've spoken. What does that path look like for you? In the past, have you hijacked your joy in relationships? Where do you need to lighten up? And where do you need to simply accept who someone is and make some community decisions from there?

CHAPTER 11

MAVERICKS AND MAGNOLIAS

I would rather have thirty minutes of
wonderful than a lifetime of nothing special.

—Shelby, *Steel Magnolias*

Y ou know those Facebook posts where you ask your friends for suggestions on what show to binge-watch next? We're always looking for that new and shiny series to hold our attention and give us something to text everyone we know, dying to talk about that oh-my-gawd twist at the end. I love diving into a new drama that reels you in and holds you there, episode after episode.

But sometimes, my mood is like that and new and shiny ain't gonna cut it. I need to curl up on the sofa and indulge in some cinematic comfort food. It's the same as the unmistakable pang I get for my momma's meat loaf, where nothing better than a ketchup-slathered slice with a side of mashed potatoes can sate my appetite. We've all got those movies and shows we have watched a hundred times and know we'll see at least another hundred before we're in the ground. It's what we watch when we need to spend an hour or two cleansing our brains from the constant go-go-go and come out refreshed and perked up on the other side.

Steel Magnolias is my Momma's meat loaf.

Funny enough, it's not the genuine depiction of Southern women and their friendships that makes me reach for this movie over and over like a warm, familiar blanket. It's that in its darkest moments, when even the coldest hearts melt enough for tears to uncontrollably flow, *Steel Magnolias* doesn't keep digging down into the pits of despair. Nope. It smacks us upside the ear with humor so unexpected that we choke on our own spit.

Hands down, my favorite scene in the entire movie is after Shelby's funeral when her mother, M'Lynn, is feeling all her pain and anguish bubble up to the surface and spill out in front of her friends. Sally Field delivers her lines as a mother tragically, so unfairly, burying her own child, with such visceral agony, oscillating between unthinkable heartache and utter fury at the unfairness of it all. She lets out her grief with exhausted whimpers, clearly having cried all the tears a mother could possibly cry. The next moment, there's a sharp inhale and M'Lynn composes herself, checking her appearance in a compact. Laughing over a memory of her daughter saying her hair looked like a brown football helmet, she falls apart again, breaking down in tears before coming back up in teeth-clenching, white-hot outrage. It's a gut-wrenching roller coaster that reduces me to a puddle without fail, every time.

Throughout it all Dolly Parton, Daryl Hannah, Shirley MacLaine, and Olympia Dukakis are trying to be there for their friend. They follow her as she paces and stomps and crumbles, screaming that she just wants to hit something and hit it hard. But it's clear that nobody knows quite what to do or say, because how do you comfort a woman who is going through the worst loss imaginable?

Well, you offer her the chance to whack her frenemy, obviously.

Out of desperation to offer any kind of relief to the friend imploding before her, Clairee, played by Olympia Dukakis, grabs Shirley MacLaine and yells at Sally Field, "Here, hit this!"

MacLaine's Ouiser is a grumpy old woman who has self-admittedly been in a bad mood for forty years. She yells at Clairee that she must be high as everyone else looks horrified by Clairee's continued unhinged encouragement of M'Lynn to "whack Ouiser." This is a once-in-a-lifetime opportunity, to slap a woman who routinely huffs and puffs, mouthing off to anyone who makes eye contact. If you're ever going to get a pass to deck someone this annoying and to do it with impunity, it would be to numb the pain of burying your child.

The absurdity of the moment breaks through and a smile softens M'Lynn's shocked expression. The whole group—minus Ouiser, who has stormed off and flipped the bird in a cemetery—dissolves into giggles. They all try to stifle their laughter, M'Lynn even covering her face with a hankie that just minutes ago had wiped away tears cried above her daughter's grave.

Every single time I watch this scene, without fail, I go from sniffling sobs to the kind of raucous laughter that makes your tummy ache and burns your lungs. Not because the idea of hitting Ouiser is in and of itself particularly hilarious. But because the moment punctuates devastation with such unexpected levity.

Dark humor is the most necessary iteration of joy. Without it, the possibility of light feels unfathomable in our darkest moments. It is proof that joy can survive.

When I first watched that movie as a child, I didn't quite understand the poignancy of that moment. It didn't make sense how somebody could laugh and cry, be joyful and grieving, how any of this could possibly coexist in the same place, comfortably. It's taken some life and some years to understand the brilliance of the juxtaposition, to understand not just why it works on-screen, but why it works in some of the darkest moments of real life. Laughter in the face of tragedy is proof that joy remains, even in the dark.

As children, we are taught that there is happy and sad; there is good and bad. Kids don't really explore the gray in between. We tend to keep the lines separated for them, making life seem a little more predictable, manageable, safe. Laughter means happy; tears mean sad. They don't need to understand dark comedy, because they haven't yet (hopefully) experienced something so dark that it needs a moment of levity. But as life goes on, we learn the blend of flavors. There is bitter in the sweet. There is laughter in the sad. There is strength in weakness. There is joy in grief. There is melancholy in the happy.

Yeah, I don't feel the need to unpack all that irony for my kids just yet. And I probably had a time in my younger life when I didn't want the coexistence of these things to be true, didn't want to acknowledge that dark levity is sometimes the best way to get through the darkest places.

But as an adult, I have.

> There is bitter in the sweet. There is laughter in the sad. There is strength in weakness. There is joy in grief. There is melancholy in the happy.

• • • • • • •

It was smack-dab in the middle of 2020, that godforsaken dumpster fire of a year, when Ian, myself, and our two best friends sat down for much-needed fellowship. Elliott and Ian worked together in the emergency department, where the pandemic had so overwhelmed their system that they were triaging in tents in the parking lot. They were emotionally exhausted from seeing so much death and frustrated from working without sufficient PPE, and on top of all that, the internet was gaslighting health-care workers, saying the virus "wasn't that bad."

Melissa was working as an ob-gyn, and her work stress was also through the roof. At the time, very little was known about COVID-19 and its impacts on pregnancy. Melissa's job was to help her patients mitigate the risk, which sounded like quite the undertaking. How do you keep a pregnant woman calm when something that scary is happening? You don't want to make them overly chill about it, because they need to take it seriously, but you don't want them fixating so much on the risk that their pregnancy turns into a nine-month-long anxiety attack.

"I'm tired," Melissa said.

"Me too," we all agreed.

While "tired" fell drastically short in capturing how we felt, it was the word we kept returning to, repeatedly, throughout the night.

"You know what I'm tired of?" Elliot asked, taking a sip of his whiskey.

"What's that?" I asked, curious how he could possibly narrow it down to one thing.

"This damn town," Elliott said with a laugh. "All of this is Fort Myers's fault, obviously. Ever since we moved here, my luck has changed. I barely remember having any. I guess I oughta move before I find out what Fort Myers is gonna take from me next!"

"I came to Fort Myers, and I had hair! Now look!" Ian rubbed his hand over his bald head, and the rest of us busted out laughing.

Melissa was watching with an eyebrow raised. Fort Myers had stolen from her, too. She leaned back in her chair and sipped on her wine, relinquishing her turn in this dark game.

"Well, I guess it's my turn then," I said, taking a sip of my drink.

"Yeah, let's hear it," Melissa said. "What has Fort Myers stolen from you?"

I didn't have to think about it. It was right there, waiting. I raised my glass and said, "My nipples."

Ian spewed his drink into the fire, and Melissa couldn't stop laughing.

"You win, MK." Elliott laughed and stopped to wipe his eyes. "Not that this is the Struggle Olympics, but if it were..."

"I know," I agreed. "I'd win."

Looking back on that moment, it's amazing to me how

hard we were able to laugh. I mean, hunkered-over, slapping-our-thighs, tears-streaming-down kind of laughter. The truth is, we were all very much in crisis, and our struggles were nothing to laugh about—and yet, we couldn't stop. We didn't *want* to. The whole thing was morbidly healing.

It was funny, too, how we jokingly decided it was best to blame everything on Fort Myers. I suppose it was nice to imagine we could just pack up and leave all our troubles. That somewhere, out there, was some shining new city—where Elliott would land a perfect job, Ian would regrow hair, and my boobs would magically Frankenstein themselves back into their precancer form.

We laughed 'til we cried, because all of it was madness—or perhaps because we were all a bit mad. I think we all felt like we'd tumbled down some rabbit hole and woken up in a world where nothing made sense. And there we were, living our lives against some whack-a-doo backdrop, wondering all along if the world was as crazy as we thought it was, or if our grasp on reality was slipping.

I've never needed a laugh like that so badly in my life. Looking around the fire, I clearly wasn't alone in that. We'd all sat in our emotional pain, our physical exhaustion, well past long enough. No hairlines or nipples were returning. If we were going down the rabbit hole, falling and falling through the endless darkness, we might as well do it laughing maniacally instead of screaming in terror.

Like that scene from *Alice in Wonderland*, where the Mad Hatter has a moment of prescience. He's in the middle of celebrating the unbirthday party, with his talking animal friends, when he stops to ask a question.

"Am I going mad?" he asks his new friend, Alice. I'm certain he knew the answer.

"I'm afraid so," said Alice. "You're entirely bonkers. But, I'll tell you a secret: All the best people are."

• • • • • • •

Of all the speed bumps we will encounter on our journeys to joy, crisis is the most unique. The thing is, we can control our thoughts on comparison. We can catch them early and shut them down. And we also have control over the communities we build, and the people we let into our lives. But when it comes to a crisis, we have zero control—it just rolls into life, uninvited. Be it death, divorce, the loss of a job, or you know, a fun new global pandemic. Crisis comes out of nowhere and looks different for everybody. So how do we protect our joy?

Well, we can't prevent it and we can't predict it, so the best we can do is prepare for it. Let me give you a good example. To the delight of my somewhat feral cat, Waffles, my backyard is jam-packed with squirrels. Our trees are plentiful, and they produce nuts and berries, so those suckers stay plump and happy year-round. But you wouldn't know that by looking out the window, because squirrels never sit still. They're always running around the yard, frantically collecting whatever sustenance they can get their little paws on. Squirrels are hoarders, which is sort of hilarious. But it's how they survive in a crisis—for instance, when their food freezes or when they're forced into hiding by a fat tuxedo cat named Waffles.

Like squirrels, we need to stock up on joy. Take every little nugget we can find and hoard it. We never know when those reserves will be needed—it happens when we least expect it. The pandemic started right before my birthday, and the world shut down with a swiftness. Everything was scary and heavy and horrible, so when my special day rolled around, I didn't say a word. Because, honestly, it just felt trivial: *Who cares that I was born? Who wants to eat cake? People are dying; this isn't important.*

In my mind, joy felt inappropriate. Like it didn't make sense in the moment. I wouldn't carry a smiley face balloon into a funeral, so I shouldn't celebrate when others are suffering.

> When we are hurting, we need to find healing: and joy is the thing we need most.

The irony in that line of thinking is it keeps us from healing. When we are hurting, we need to find healing: and joy is the thing we need most. There are hundreds of studies that show the physiological effects of stress are seriously damaging to our health. And studies have also shown that little moments of joy can literally help us recover from that stress.

The thing is, joy exists for a reason—both scientifically and spiritually speaking. It's not just the powdered sugar of life; take it or leave it, your preference. It doesn't exist just to sprinkle on top of things to make them sweeter.

Joy is written into our DNA. It's essential for surviving *and* thriving. If we lose joy, we've lost every good thing that reminds us to keep on living.

· · · · · · ·

Growing up, I was a crazy horse girl. Everybody knows at least one, right? Horse girls are the ones who collect Breyer ponies, who watch every horse movie known to man, who can run on all fours faster than they can run on two feet. Horse girls are the ones who grow up, and still have this very specific fantasy of encountering an unrideable horse, saying, "Let me ride that horse," and everyone in the crowd rolls their eyes because they almost died trying. And then she jumps on that horse's back and rides off into the wind all effortlessly. Anyone who doubted her watches in stunned disbelief, their mouths agape.

"Wow! She's so spectacular." Or something like that. Maybe it's just me?

Anyways, I was a horse girl. And every time family movie night rolled around, I went straight for the VHS tape with a horse on the box. The story didn't matter. Not in the least. The movie was simply a vessel, and it swiftly transported me to a world of euphoric escape, on the back of a horse. I'll occasionally watch *The Black Stallion* if I'm sick or home without kids. I don't know why. It's like a Zoom date with horses. A little virtual encounter with joy.

All that to say, I walked into the house yesterday and my husband was sitting on the couch. He was cozied up under a blanket, wide-eyed and in awe, looking very much like a second-grade horse girl. I asked him what he was watching, and he told me it was a movie called *Chasing Mavericks*.

The vibe looked suspiciously familiar to me. The free-spirited journey, the one true rider thing, the "I'm the only one who can do it" energy. He was totally having a Zoom date with joy.

"OMG!" I squealed with delight. "It's the grown-man version of a horse movie!"

Ian giggled but didn't deny it. I stole his blanket and joined him on the couch. Listen, y'all. I don't care what the Rotten Tomatoes says, *Chasing Mavericks* is a damn good movie.

It's based on the true story of the late surfing phenom Jay Moriarity. The movie starts when Jay is just fifteen years old. He's a young surfer who incidentally discovers that the mythic Mavericks surf break actually existed and was near his home in California. Mavericks is considered one of the biggest waves on earth, so naturally, Jay is determined to conquer it. He enlists the help of Frosty Hesson, a local legend and Mavericks survivor who is incidentally played by a *very* surfable Gerard Butler. As Jay and Frosty carry on their quest to achieve the impossible, they develop a unique friendship that transforms both their lives. Hesson teaches Jay to surf Mavericks, and he goes on to wipe out in such epic fashion that it earns him the cover of *Surfer* magazine.

You see, training for Mavericks wasn't just about the ability to ride a big wave. Jay Moriarity was already a big-wave surfer. Training for Mavericks meant learning to navigate two specific dangerous conditions unique to the break itself. Mavericks is difficult to surf for two reasons. One, it requires a significant amount of speed while maneuvering around dangerous clusters of rock. So, lesson one is avoiding the skull-crushing rocks. And two, there's a spot in Mavericks that is essentially just a chaotic wall of white water. So lesson two is how to stay out of the wash.

If you are dumped out of a wave and get "caught inside," you could potentially end up in this wall of white water that behaves like the world's biggest literal washing machine. Survival training for Mavericks meant learning to hold your breath for several minutes at a time. I hate to spoil the movie for you, but you probably already know where this is headed.

Jay gets stuck in the wash, spun around like a load of dirty blue jeans.

Now, according to Hollywood this was about three minutes long, and while I was watching I have to tell you, it felt more like ten. When Jay's board popped up in two different pieces, and he didn't emerge shortly after, every second felt like a punch in the gut. The crowd didn't think he would make it. In true Hollywood fashion (but also in real life), Jay popped up, smiling and unbeaten. He even grabbed his backup board and paddled once again out to the break.

• • • • • • •

Can you imagine the sound of that ragged breath? That desperate gasp for air after getting stuck in the wash for three minutes? I can tell you right now, after fifteen seconds under, I would pop out of the water, sucking so loudly for air, you'd think a human-sized vacuum had just picked up some marbles.

The body doesn't care what it looks or sounds like when it's desperately trying to get oxygen. When it comes down to it, we want to survive. We have instincts to keep on living.

And this is exactly why I believe we are tempted to find moments of levity in the thick of a crisis. It's your joy, kicking up out of the water, trying to come up for air. When things are heavy, and scary, or bleak…it's that ragged gasp for joy. Sure, dark humor is weird and a little uncomfortable, but you know what? The soul doesn't care what it looks like when it's gasping for oxygen, either. It's why your cousin cracks that joke about how weird your grandma looked when she was in the coffin. It's why I joke that my nipple-free, postmastectomy boobs make me look like a character from *Gumby*. It's why Clairee told M'Lynn that she should take a whack at Ouiser, and why we laughed and sobbed right along with her.

Our bodies aren't the only things with a killer survival instinct. It turns out, our joy fights like hell to survive this life, as well. But here's the difference between our souls and the surfers:

You see, surfers can choose their waves.

They can train for Mavericks and build up resilience and practice holding their breath. They can decide if they want to risk the wash for the waves, or if they would rather just float in the lineup. They train for the amount of risk that they choose. Big waves means big minutes underwater. But the best surfers are usually the craziest. It takes a certain kind of edge to survive those waves, never mind jumping in them for fun.

The difference is our souls don't get to determine our breaks. Our souls don't get to mitigate risk. One day is smooth sailing and the next day is Mavericks, and that's just the way life goes. We have no idea where this journey will take us, but we know we want to have joy. And well, if that's what you want, then you must build resilience for the days when crises will come. Underwater, you have to hold your breath.

But in a crisis, we have to practice something else: holding on to our joy.

• • • • • • •

I was eight when my first pet bit the dust. I hopped off the bus and was greeted by my sister's tabby cat. She was fat and happy, purring like a freaking freight train. I scratched her between her ears and headed inside to hold my canary, Pickles.

It was eerily quiet on our screened porch. No tweets or whistles. I spotted the empty cage and proceeded to scan the perimeter. Pickles couldn't have gotten far…her wings were clipped.

A few green feathers floated from the ceiling.

"Mooooom!?"

Mom walked into the room, drying her hands on her blue jeans.

"Oh, honey. I'm so sorry. Pickles flew away today. I saw her in the backyard playing with some robins, though. She seemed happy."

Somewhere outside, that damn cat was cleaning her chops.

Years later, I would unearth the truth about that day. Mom had just finished crime scene cleanup when I got home from school, wiping God-knows-what off on her blue jeans. She explained gently that there was nothing she could do, and she thought I'd be happier imagining my bird hanging out with the neighborhood fowl.

"Pickles didn't even get a proper burial!" I flung my arms up with emphasis. "You could've at least kept her body for me!"

Mom did not challenge my dramatic antics. She did not mention the fact that there wasn't enough bird left for a shoebox. There isn't anyone on earth, besides a mom, that wouldn't put their foot down squarely over the idea of preserving a feathery corpse. Instead, she looked me dead in the eye and said, "I'll keep that in mind next time. Promise."

• • • • • • •

When I was twelve, we got a cockatiel named Max. That bird was awesome. He pooped on my shoulder, smelled like rotten oatmeal, and bit my finger. Naturally, I adored him.

Late one evening I returned home from summer vacation. Exhausted, I dropped my bags and went straight to bed. I didn't notice the silence. Or the empty cage. Or the feathers.

I slept, happily oblivious.

The next morning I plugged in the toaster and opened the freezer to grab a waffle.

"Jesus, Mary, and Joseph!!"

There was Max, propped up inside an innocuous Eggo box. Stiff as a feathered British soldier, beady little eyes staring straight ahead at the frozen corn. I poked him to be sure I wasn't seeing things. He was hard as a rock.

"MOOOOM! Mom-mom-mom!"

"Oh, no," I heard my mother murmur upon entering the kitchen. "Honey, I was going to tell you last night, but…"

"Why is Max in the freezer, Mom? He's frozen stiff! Next to the freakin' waffles! What happened?!"

Mom thought I'd want to bury his body.

She'd kept me in mind.

I was too freaked out to even respond. I left my waffle on the counter and fled to my room, slamming the door behind me. I mean, it takes a little while to process something like that. It's not every day that you go scrounging for breakfast and come up with a cockatiel carcass instead.

Max's funeral was a beautiful event. We lowered him into the ground (next to my brother's late guinea pig Spike, R.I.P.) as a cassette tape played the *Braveheart* soundtrack. And kudos to Momma, he was well-preserved for the whole affair.

As a child, I regularly wondered about my mother's sanity. Her hair was a little wild. Our dinners were creative, so to speak (Shrek meat loaf). She made more than a few bizarre parenting choices in the early '90s, but hey, I didn't die. And looking back on things now, I'm beginning to understand her more. And what I'm coming to understand is that her life had some Mavericks, for real. There were times when she was fighting to get back up for air, and as a child I didn't know it. What I saw then was green meat loaf and wild hair and Max in a waffle-box coffin, but this is what I see now when I look at my mom:

A survivor.

Someone who knows how to fight for joy, how to hang on to it, even in the midst of the Mavericks. I see someone who tried to find humor in every situation, who learned how to hold her breath, and her joy, and who got caught in the wash, over and over again, but managed to pop back up, smiling.

• • • • • • •

I have the distinct privilege of being married to a soul surfer, but lemme tell you, he's a weird brand of human. It's like there's a billion tiny magnets embedded in Ian's DNA, constantly tugging his heart toward the ocean. His mind and his body are never far behind. I know this because, at any given time, he has twenty browser tabs open on his computer, and all of them are checking the waves of some beach, somewhere he wishes he were. If Ian could make his bed in the ocean, I'm convinced he would. Which, I suppose, is why he wants to be buried at sea. The joy of the ocean calls out to him. It calls out for deep eternity, and perhaps that's what it means to be a soul surfer.

I will never forget the day I realized how deeply that joy was embedded. Ian and I were visiting Cocoa Beach, back before we had children. We loved visiting the pier; Ian would surf for hours and I'd read a book in the shade. We'd get there at sunrise and he'd surf 'til dark, then we'd grab burgers and drive back home.

I was surprised during one trip when it wasn't even noon, and Ian emerged from the water. He set his board in the sand beside me and plopped down in an empty chair.

"Everything okay, babe?" I asked, looking up from my book.

"Oh yeah, the waves are awesome," he replied. "Just taking a little break."

Quick note on soul surfers: They don't get tired. This is a physiological fact. They stop surfing when they run out of waves or sunshine—and Ian had plenty of both. I suspected something was amiss. I glanced out at the water, and wouldn't you know it, every other surfer was "on a break," too.

"Is there a shark out there, Ian?"

Ian smiled sheepishly. "I didn't want you to worry," he said.

And wouldn't you know, I was right. There was a six-foot hammerhead shark snacking on baitfish just beyond the break. I looked around the sand, half hoping, half expecting to see all the surfers packing up to go home. But no. They were scattered around the beach, boards in hand, just waiting to paddle back out. And I'm telling you, it wasn't ten minutes later, that's exactly what they did.

Turns out, there's more to being a soul surfer than finding one's joy in the sea. It's about embracing a healthy understanding of fear; it's growing comfortable with an element of risk. Every surfer knows that there's more to the ocean than a set of well-formed waves. There's the undertow, white water, rip currents, and shore breaks, to say nothing of hammerhead sharks. With all that risk, it's hard to imagine any sane person paddling out.

And it dawns on me, *this* is what joy does. It nurtures a spirit of defiance in the face of crushing adversity. It reminds your soul that it's not time to quit, not now, and it keeps you fighting. Joy is countercultural, as well. It won't make sense from the shore. If you pursue it, if you fight to protect it, there will be a million dissenting voices.

Believe me, friend, there are detractors of joy who will beckon you to stay on the sand. And some of those people might even be your loved ones, who are scared by the height of the waves.

Joy isn't found in safe, predictable places. In fact, in my experience, it shows up where you'd least expect it. It is raucous when people think it should be quiet. It's quietly content when the world demands it can be found only in partying. It's happily surfing a glittering wave, alongside a hammerhead shark.

In some seasons, joy seems easily found. In others, it's a difficult hunt. Sometimes it can be cradled lightly in your hands, and sometimes you hold it like your last breath of air, as you cycle beneath the waves.

But crazy joy is looking at the foamy wild of the ocean and saying, "I'm going to surf those waves. And when I wipe out, because I will, I'm going to hold on to joy. And when I get caught in the wash, because I will, I'm going to fight to come up for air. And come hell or literal high water, if I pop back up, I'm gonna paddle back out to the break."

TOUR GUIDE TAKEAWAYS

- Someone fighting for joy might look very different than your average bear. They might traverse different paths, laugh at weird times, walk barefoot when the rest of the world is laced up. Who have you known that was persevering in joy in spite of tough circumstances? Perhaps with off-the-beaten-path behavior or unconventional means? What do you learn about joy from their life?

- And let me ask you this: That thing you've had on a leash, that thing you've named Joy and made a tag for, is it really Joy? Or is it something else?

- Pursuing crazy joy means we have to go over some wild terrain. It means we'll find joy in the most unexpected places. Where is joy leading you that you've been hesitant to go? Where is joy taking you that you know will require some risk, some loss, some readjustment, some better self-advocacy?

- Which leads to this: Are you ready, really ready, to let joy take the lead? Whatever adjustment, whatever therapy, whatever meds, whatever God asks? Are you ready to go there?

CHAPTER 12

LIFE IN THE UPSIDE DOWN

Fear is healthy; panic is deadly.
—Frosty Hesson

Have you ever watched *Stranger Things?* It's a show about a group of kids in 1980s small-town Hawkins, Indiana, who uncover a supernatural underbelly to the seemingly ordinary world around them. When one of the kids, Will, disappears on a nighttime bike ride home from a Dungeons & Dragons game, his friends set out to find him. Eventually, they discover that Will has been captured by a monster and is trapped in the Upside Down, an alternate dimension that mirrors ours but is inhospitable to human life. The Upside Down is dark, cold, and covered in a goo that connects all living things in it to the Mind Flayer, an all-powerful entity bent on human destruction and taking over the world.

The Upside Down is our world, but upside down. In it are all the same places that we have in our world, but it is absent human life and most notably, joy. The Upside Down is the opposite of life, the opposite of anything good. Even though Will manages to survive while trapped there, he is consumed by fear and sadness, and is desperate to escape. He knows there is no life for him or any other human being in this bleak, haunting world.

Throughout the series, the gate to the Upside Down is opened and closed over and over. The Mind Flayer is supposedly defeated over and over. And yet, the gate between worlds is always reopened and that evil creature continues to find its way back to the people of Hawkins. It keeps finding ways to suck them back into the Upside Down.

Wrapped up in a blanket on my couch, the parallels between our world and the Upside Down struck me. Not in terms of the landscape or even the color palette, but how it relates to the human experience. It suddenly occurred to me that the Upside Down is trauma. It doesn't discriminate; it comes for the old, young, rich, and poor. The people in this otherwise unremarkable town escape it time after time. And yet, at the least likely times or places, they end up right back in that dark and desolate universe. They become surrounded by absence—of the people they love, of the homes they know, and of hope.

The show gives off some very strong *E.T.*, Spielbergian

vibes that triggered my '80s-kid nostalgia right off the bat. It's not just that every kid in Hawkins rides their bike everywhere and that the '80s are the last time I can remember that being a thing kids did freely and away from the watchful eye of adults. It's not even the disturbing pervasiveness of haircuts that look like bangs going all the way around the head. If Gen Z brings that look back, I am handing in my resignation. No, it's that the story revolves around a group of kids who go on a perilous adventure and still manage to come out kids before the credits roll.

The kids in *Stranger Things* can fight off terrifying monsters and thwart evil plans left and right, and somehow still manage to be petrified by the social dynamics of a school dance. They've seen and been through unspeakable horror, and then they return to doing the things they love, like playing arcade games or putting together elaborate D&D campaigns. They maintain their desire to experience joy.

Stranger Things reminds me of how trauma can come into our lives and wreak havoc, but it doesn't get to win. Our desire to feel joy in all things, our instinct to seek out the light, will always be more powerful than our susceptibility to darkness. It may not always feel that way, and there are certainly instances when we need time for our instincts and desires to awaken after trauma does its worst. But that light is not extinguished. The gate back to our world may be difficult to find and feel impossible to make our way back to. But it does not close.

• • • • • • •

My original plan was to end this book by exploring the pursuit of joy. Chasing joy and finally capturing it is the whole point, right?

Wrong.

There is an element crucial to joy that we haven't discussed yet, and I have a feeling it may surprise you. The essential element, missing from the equation many of us follow in our own journey to joy, is fear.

Fear is a crucial element of joy. Not terror or panic, though we'll get to those in a minute. Fear.

I love the beach. The smell of the salty air. The sounds of waves crashing against the shore. Pulling a sandwich and an ice-cold coke out of the cooler. My kids are finally at an age when I can watch them from my chair, book in my lap, while they build sandcastles and chase their boogie boards. I've loved it since I was a child myself, so sharing this special place with my babies and watching them form their own bonds with the ocean must be how parents feel cheering on their favorite baseball team with their little ones.

My love for all things beach took a brief hiatus when I was in elementary school, though.

Most of us have seen *Jaws*. At the very least, we know the ominous John Williams *duh-nuh* score that alerts even the most oblivious among us that danger is hurtling in our direction. I remember seeing *Jaws* as a child and Steven Spielberg's robo-shark-monster having the exact impression you think it would on a person still hanging on to a few baby teeth. By 2022 standards, letting me watch was not a stellar parenting choice, but I fault the nineties more than my own mother. We all made it out of that decade having consumed a lot of media that wasn't even a little appropriate for our innocent eyes and ears. Most of it didn't scar us for life and we can still look back on our childhood movies and music fondly. But after seeing this homicidal shark terrorize a whole town *and* Richard Dreyfuss, I vowed to never dip so much as a pinky toe into the Gulf of Mexico again.

Of course, I'm not the only person who had that reaction. Lots of people were either scared away from the ocean or hunted sharks under the assumption they were making people safer. So many that Peter Benchley, the author whose book the movie is based on, regretted writing it in the first place. *Jaws* was so frightening that panic set in as people were suddenly aware of this danger swimming just below the water's surface. Countless people who deeply enjoyed their trips to the beach now felt so afraid of the possibility of a shark encounter they wouldn't go near it. Their fear robbed them of this experience that had consistently brought them so much joy.

If joy is the ocean, what is keeping us from truly experiencing joy? It isn't the shark, I promise. The shark has always been there. It's fear. The *Jaws* effect. The idea that something bad *could* happen and how that idea loops in our heads and becomes all-consuming. Fear becomes less of a healthy regulator and moves on to controlling our lives. Fear should be an instinct we give a nod to and consider when making choices.

But how many of us wind up letting our fear take the wheel, steering us toward its whims and away from our own?

> How many of us wind up letting our fear take the wheel, steering us toward its whims and away from our own?

The collective response to the existence of sharks after *Jaws* was pure panic. Panic is not rational. Panic makes us do dumb things like swearing off one of the few places I could feel happy and carefree. Not that *Jaws* shouldn't have given me any trepidation about what's lurking in the dark salt water. A little fear is the normal, rational response to the idea that sharks are swimming around a public beach, hungry for human flesh. But too much fear kept me (and a whole mess of grown adults) from considering that there are no murderous sharks stalking small towns to chow down on its children and naked coeds. Shark attacks were and are extremely rare. The odds that I would run into my beloved ocean and be noticed, let alone gobbled up, by a great white are so infinitely small that there should have never been even a hesitation to get back in the water.

There is a life for you out there that is happy. It's a safe life. It's *fine*. The risk in that life is small, but so is the reward. You can stay in the shallow water for fear of what might happen if you venture further out. There is nothing inherently wrong about wading in the shallow end, always being able to touch your toes to the bottom. You can float there until your hands are pruney and settle for being happy.

But if you crave joy, you eventually must paddle out and assume some risk in its pursuit. I had to psych myself up to get back in the water after my time with Brody, Quint, and Hooper. Do I keep an eye out for a lone fin cutting through the water? Occasionally. Fear is still there. But the reward of joy—of feeling my body weightlessly bobbing with the waves—grew larger than my perceived risk.

Like the day Ian swam back into the ocean after seeing a hammerhead shark—I thought he was crazy.

But that's the thing: Joy *is* crazy. In the face of heartache, mortality, risk, and time, it doesn't make sense. Joy is defiant against the backdrop of suffering that accompanies the human experience. But that's exactly why we need it. In a world that's perpetually upside down, it is joy that holds us up. It is joy that gives us a sense of peace

> In a world that's perpetually upside down, it is joy that holds us up.

and strength in a time of crisis. When the sun goes dark and the world grows cold, happiness can wither like a fading iris.

And in those times, we will need something to reach for. We need delight that can outlast the winter. We need laughter and friendship and self-compassion. We need peace that can weather the storm.

Our crazy, resilient joy.

> We need delight that can outlast the winter. We need laughter and friendship and self-compassion. We need peace that can weather the storm.

. . . .

TOUR GUIDE TAKEAWAYS

It's hard to define a thing like joy. Our language falls painfully short. It's so much bigger than fleeting happiness, far more abstract than emotion. It's a richness of life that puts fire in your eyes and gives you the strength to keep going.

But how do you know if you're on the right path? That your journey is bending toward joy? Well, you have to start reading the signs. If your journey is marked with contentment, hope, and peace, you're on the right path. If your journey is marked by chaos and discontent, then, friend, it's time to pull over.

To find that crazy kind of joy, you have to be listening for its call—and it sounds like deep, deep eternity. I'll give you a hint: These things are simple. Curating your joy costs nothing. There's joy to be found in loving your people. Joy in loving yourself. There's joy in the laughter of your children, joy in hymns at your church. There's joy in the taste of your momma's peach cobbler. Joy in the rustling leaves. It's in every relationship, every place, every moment you wish could stretch into forever.

There's a reason that joy calls out for eternity. Because joy is a whisper from God. It's our compass needle that points true north in moments when life is most pure. Joy, I believe, is what points us to heaven, reminding us where we belong. What I want for you, for all of us, is a joy that calls out for eternity. So if you want to know if you're on the right path, then look at the compass within.

Because the journey to joy bends straight up to heaven, the place where God answers its call.

. . . .

ACKNOWLEDGMENTS

Mike Salisbury, my amazing agent. You are the Mando to my Grogu. Thanks for watching out for me in this crazy world of publishing. The week that *Holy Hot Mess* was released, I called Mike in tears. Nothing was going as planned, I said. The whole thing was a holy, hot mess. Mike laughed and told me his theory on publishing...more like a superstition, I guess. Apparently, the title of your book is how your publishing process will go. Still...I went with *Crazy Joy* this time. And Mike was right, as usual (eye roll).

Let me start by thanking the phenomenal team who helped bring this book to life. It has more than lived up to its title, hasn't it? I couldn't have done it without you.

Thank you, thank you, thank you:

Mike Salisbury, for constantly being in my corner. I can't decide if you're a better agent or friend; it's amazing how you manage to be both.

To Karen, Curtis, and Sealy: I'm so proud to be part of the Yates & Yates family. Thank you for not firing me, yet.

Karen Longino, for flinging open every door that I've been

lucky enough to walk through. We are long overdue for a trip to the beach. First margarita on me.

Patsy, for playing bodyguard when that sloppy frat guy kept following me around at a book signing, and for going to bat against that sketchy newspaper. I never once doubted that I was on *your* list.

Laini and Cat, for being marketing and publicity gurus who get my words before readers. I adore you as much as sriracha.

Julie Lyles Carr, my writing doula, for delivering this book in the back of a van flying ninety miles an hour toward a deadline.

Sara Farrell Baker, it's so rare to find someone who also speaks dolphin. Thank you for being that person. And thank you for editing with me 'til two in the morning while I cried that everything was garbage. You took my meh and made it marvelous. I love you more than Lin-Manuel Miranda.

Brina, Miss Stompy Boots, for running my show. You make my life easier as a colleague, and you make my life happier as a friend. So pretty much, my life is better because you're in it. I love you.

Hannah Banana, there just aren't words. Being your friend is way too easy; you aren't allowed to ever leave. Also, if you do, I have way too much blackmail material. So boom. You're stuck with me, forever.

To Mon, Lauren, and KK. What would I do without you three? Your love and support are always one call away, and I feel it from way over here. Thank you for always covering my back, for loving me well, and for not publishing the Batman videos that I insisted you film in landscape.

And to Worthy Books for taking my words and putting them out into the world.

Now for the people who, for some strange reason, continue to love me for free...

Thank you...

Ian: For loving me well. You're my best friend, my confidant, my partner in crime. I can't believe I was lucky enough to find you. Sixteen years, and I still follow you around our house like a golden retriever. Thanks for never making it weird. I love you so much it hurts.

Ben and Holland: My love for you stretches into eternity. You two are my craziest joys.

Momma: No matter how many times you say you love me, I love you three times more. Thanks for being my constant presence in this crazy, upside-down world. It says everything that nearly every story I write begins with "Momma..."

Sis: If I could write into existence the perfect sister, it would literally be you. I love you so much, and you'll always be my hero, even though you lied about the unicorns in the closet. Water under the bridge.

Tyrone the Horrible: I don't know how it's even possible, but we've gotten closer with age. I'm sorry about the ghost stories, and for using your bunk bed as a bug mausoleum. You know I'll always have your back, even if you wreck Momma's BMW and try to put it back together with duct tape (ahem).

Daddy: If I ever get arrested, you'll be my first call. Thank you for being that person. I've always known you would answer my call and love me no matter what.

And thank you to my readers, for keeping me employed and for laughing at my weird sense of humor. Especially the one who lives in Texas, who drove to multiple bookstores and moved all my books to the Best Sellers shelf. They totally thought it was me who did it, but I don't care.

I love you for it.

ABOUT THE AUTHOR

Mary Katherine Backstrom is the national bestselling author of *Holy Hot Mess,* and she is also known for her viral videos and candid writing on family, faith, and mental illness. She has been featured on the *TODAY* show and CNN, and in the *New York Times*—but her friends and family are most impressed with her onetime appearance on *Ellen.* MK resides in Alabama with her husband, children, two dogs, and a cat. When she isn't writing, MK is active in her church, her community, and her favorite Mexican restaurant.